Autoethnography, Self-Narrative and Teacher Education

STUDIES IN PROFESSIONAL LIFE AND WORK

Volume 5

Editor
Ivor Goodson
Education Research Centre, University of Brighton, UK

Editorial Board
J. M. Pancheco, *University of Minho, Portugal*
David Labaree, *Stanford University*
Sverker Lindblad, *University of Gothenburg*
Leslie Siskin, *NYU/Steinhardt Institute for Education & Social Policy*

Scope
The series will commission books in the broad area of professional life and work. This is a burgeoning area of study now in educational research with more and more books coming out on teachers' lives and work, on nurses' life and work, and on the whole interface between professional knowledge and professional lives.

The focus on life and work has been growing rapidly in the last two decades. There are a number of rationales for this. Firstly, there is a methodological impulse: many new studies are adopting a life history approach. The life history tradition aims to understand the interface between people's life and work and to explore the historical context and the socio-political circumstances in which people's professional life and work is located. The growth in life history studies demands a series of books which allow people to explore this methodological focus within the context of professional settings.

The second rationale for growth in this area is a huge range of restructuring initiatives taking place throughout the world. There is in fact a world movement to restructure education and health. In most forms this takes the introduction of more targets, tests and tables and increasing accountability and performativity regimes. These initiatives have been introduced at governmental level – in most cases without detailed consultation with the teaching and nursing workforces. As a result there is growing evidence of a clash between people's professional life and work missions and the restructuring initiatives which aim to transform these missions. One way of exploring this increasingly acute clash of values is through studies of professional life and work. Hence the European Commission, for instance, have begun to commission quite large studies of professional life and work focussing on teachers and nurses. One of these projects – the Professional Knowledge Network project has studied teachers' and nurses' life and work in seven countries. There will be a range of books coming out from this project and it is intended to commission the main books on nurses and on teachers for this series.

The series will begin with a number of works which aim to define and delineate the field of professional life and work. One of the first books 'Investigating the Teacher's Life and Work' by Ivor Goodson will attempt to bring together the methodological and substantive approaches in one book. This is something of a 'how to do' book in that it looks at how such studies can be undertaken as well as what kind of generic findings might be anticipated.

Future books in the series might expect to look at either the methodological approach of studying professional life and work or provide substantive findings from research projects which aim to investigate professional life and work particularly in education and health settings.

Autoethnography, Self-Narrative and Teacher Education

Mike Hayler
University of Brighton, UK

UMass Dartmouth

Department of
Educational Leadership

Educational Leadership
and Policy Studies
Doctoral Program

SENSE PUBLISHERS
ROTTERDAM/BOSTON/TAIPEI

A C.I.P. record for this book is available from the Library of Congress.

ISBN: 978-94-6091-670-0 (paperback)
ISBN: 978-94-6091-671-7 (hardback)
ISBN: 978-94-6091-672-4 (e-book)

Published by: Sense Publishers,
P.O. Box 21858,
3001 AW Rotterdam,
The Netherlands
www.sensepublishers.com

Printed on acid-free paper

All Rights Reserved © 2011 Sense Publishers

No part of this work may be reproduced, stored in a retrieval system, or transmitted in any form or by any means, electronic, mechanical, photocopying, microfilming, recording or otherwise, without written permission from the Publisher, with the exception of any material supplied specifically for the purpose of being entered and executed on a computer system, for exclusive use by the purchaser of the work.

TABLE OF CONTENTS

List of acronyms	vii
1. Introduction	1
2. Initial teacher education and autoethnography	5
3. Conducting the research	35
4. Neighbouring voices	51
5. A story full of stories	63
6. Some conclusions	97
Appendix 1: Chronology of selected major events in teacher education, 1960–2010	111
Appendix 2: Method of existential psychoanalysis	115

LIST OF ACRONYMS

List of acronyms:

ATO:	Area Training Organisation
CPD:	Continuing Professional Development
DES:	Department of Education and Science
DfES:	Department for Education and Skills
DfE:	Department for Education
DfEE:	Department for Education and Employment
FE:	Further Education
FWWCP:	Federation of Worker Writers and Community Publishers
GTP:	Graduate Teacher Programme
HE:	Higher Education
HEI:	Higher Education Institution
HESA:	Higher Education Statistics Agency
HMCI:	Her Majesty's Chief Inspector
ITE:	Initial Teacher Education
ITT:	Initial Teacher Training
NQT:	Newly Qualified Teacher
OFSTED:	Office for Standards in Education Children's Services and Schools
PGCE:	Post Graduate Certificate in Education
QTS:	Qualified Teacher Status
RTP:	Registered Teacher Programme
SCITT:	School Centred Initial Teacher Training
S-STEP:	Self Study of Teacher Education Practices
TDA:	Training and Development Agency

CHAPTER 1

INTRODUCTION

THE TELLING TALE

My parents had faith in education. It worked for them. They gained qualifications at school and trained as nurses. They met in Brighton where they had gone to complete their training in 1950. They liked reading and discussion and going to see plays and they believed that education was the route towards a better life for individuals and a better society for all. They were part of the post-war consensus which supported the welfare state. They voted for the Labour party and described themselves as socialists. My eldest brother was assessed as having learning difficulties during the early years of school and attended a special school from the age of seven. My other brother did well at primary school, passed the eleven-plus and went to a technical school. I started at a state nursery school at the age of 3 in 1963. There seems to have been a bit of a problem from the start. The only real memory I have of being there is the day the teacher gave me the job of painting something. I'm not sure what it was but it was made of wood and I remember the praise that she gave me for doing such a good job all day and how pleased my Mum was that I had been good that day. This was obviously unusual although I cannot remember the 'bad' days or getting into trouble at that time. Mum says now that I was pretty active and got easily bored and that some of the others may have 'led me astray.'

This book is a study of the professional identity of university-based teacher educators in England. It is based upon my doctoral thesis research project which emerged from my personal, professional experience of working as a teacher educator in a university school of education. The study took an auto-ethnographic approach to examine my own narrative of experience alongside those of six other teacher educators. My intention was and is to illuminate the ways in which memory of our own experiences influences how we work with students who are preparing to become teachers. A key assumption underpinning the thesis and this book is that valuable insights into the work and identity of teacher educators can be gained by examining our own memories and beliefs and that the narrative discourses through which we understand ourselves and our work are a source of rich description and insight.

The processes by which we construct memory and the ways in which it informs practice are central themes here where 'Telling' works as both verb and adjective in relation to narrative tales of experience. Kierkegaard (1938) argued that while we can only live our lives forwards we can only understand them backwards. The principal purpose of this book is to investigate how we articulate our own selfhood as educators of teachers through narrative and how this informs and develops our professional

CHAPTER 1

identities which we construct and re-construct in response to the continuing uncertainties and ambivalences within the initial education of teachers in England.

This raises a number of questions about what it means to be a university-based teacher educator in England during the first decades of the 21st Century. The book examines these questions through a number of themes which arose from the writing and sharing of self-narratives and interviews with six teacher educators with the focus of the study moving between how we use memories of experience to construct and perceive our own identities as teacher-educators; how this influences our practice; and how we adapt our personal pedagogies in order to negotiate external and institutional requirements and constraints which often contradict our own beliefs about teaching and learning.

I used various types of auto-ethnography such as narrative self-study writing and life history interviews as a lens with which to examine aspects of the memories, perspectives and experiences of university-based teacher educators such as how we came to be teacher educators, what it is like to be a teacher educator, how we see our role, why we believe what we believe about initial teacher education and how we think this, all of this, affects our practice and the practice of the students of teaching and learning with whom we work. These themes are picked up through discussion of both related literature and methodology and then through the narrative analysis and organisation of Chapter 5. I chose to use the analytic auto-ethnographic approach suggested by Anderson (2006) with a method of analysis based upon the progressive/regressive method proposed by Sartre (1963) which is discussed in Chapter 2.

The focus of this book is upon teacher educators who work in university schools of education partly because that is where my experience lies as a student and a tutor and also because I believe this remains one of the most important, contested and yet under-researched areas within education. The term 'teacher education' remains itself an area of significant dispute that to some extent represents the trends and developments of three decades of reform. While there is a growing body of research into the education and training of teachers, the voices of teacher educators themselves have until recently been largely absent from this literature.

A related and equally relevant purpose has been to contribute towards professional knowledge by using, developing, examining and evaluating a method of inquiry which began from the process of writing (Richardson 2000). I wanted to develop a research method where my own auto-biographical writing was shared and responded to by other participants as a method of exploring the ways in which professional lives develop. This in turn raises issues about the way people story and use memory, the role of others in the construction of identity through narrative and the nature of professionalism.

As Kurt Lewin put it 'There's nothing more practical than a good theory' (Lewin, 1952 p169). This is especially pertinent for me in adopting definitions of professionalism where identity as formed by reflection and narratives of the self have a central role. To make these links clear requires some close examination of the areas in question and a consideration of my motives in the spirit of self-study and narrative inquiry.

INTRODUCTION

'YOU DON'T WANT TO DO IT LIKE THAT DO YOU?'

Well yes I did although I recognise that marrying together an examination of teacher education from the perspective of teacher educators with and through a collection of methods which come under the heading of autoethnography itself represents a sort of self-narrative which tells the story within the story that links my own experiences of writing, life history work and teacher education as a student, a teacher and a teacher educator. This could be the story of me trying to practise what I teach.

Freire (1972) called upon his student collaborators to take possession of their learning as one of the steps towards taking possession of their lives and so I take possession of my experience here and try to make sense of it to explain how and why I got to a certain point in my research and where I wanted to go from there.

In 2004 having been a primary school teacher for 15 years I returned as a senior lecturer to the school of education where I had gained my qualified teacher status and where I was now in the early stages of the EdD. I was so glad to be there. It seemed like a dream job after a tough few years teaching children identified as having emotional and behavioural difficulties. Over the three years I worked at the unversity some of my own emotional and behavioural difficulties re-emerged and I felt increasingly as though I was acting, pretending to be someone else, saying one thing and doing another. My professed pedagogy did not match my actual practice which contradicted some of my deeply held beliefs at certain points. I felt like a fraud and as though everyone could see straight through me. While I felt my own confidence as a teacher draining away in what could be explained as professional menopause or a mid-life crisis as I approached 50, it was my growing doubt within and questions about the enterprise of teacher education itself that seemed to be feeding this most actively. My feelings of not being authentic and doubts about the authenticity of my profession led to anxiety and confusion and brought memories and feelings to the surface that had been buried long ago.

This feeling of dissonance was further compounded by the difficulty I was having in examining these questions, memories and doubts by 'getting back to' my work on my doctoral study which seemed to be slipping further and further away from me. I resigned from the job in an attempt to regain some sense of equilibrium by completing the Doctorate and working out what to do next. I wanted to read, listen, talk and write myself out of trouble and regain a sense of authenticity in my work. It had all got so complicated. Once upon a time when I had lived a different sort of life it seems in my memory at least that all that was required was to improve upon the blank page (Hayler, 2003). In some ways the blank page is perfect as it is: uncomplicated, unchallenging, and uncontroversial. Once you make your mark and begin to tell a tale of who you are things can seem to both open up and narrow down at the same time. You play your hand, reveal yourself and begin that story in one way or another. I had learnt of course that the invisible ink of expectation is always upon the page and I was interested to know where that came from.

Why stories? That is pretty much how I understand writing whatever the subject, the form or the style. As a reader I need to know where a poem 'is' and

3

CHAPTER 1

what it does. I read research journals as narratives and search, sometimes in vain, for the voice within and behind the 'findings' and the analysis. To me this is the real 'synthesis,' a word much beloved by the authors of Higher Education assessment criteria: the coming together and connecting of information, ideas and theories within the experience and mind of the writer and then hopefully upon the no-longer blank page. I don't mean by this that I only read fiction although to some extent all writing is a form of fiction of course. It can only aspire towards truth in its various forms. All writing is by definition 'creative', all reading as Denzin says, 'interpretive' (2001). What I mean is that the writing that I understand best, my favourite 'non-fiction', is often in the form of very definite narratives which take the reader through the labyrinth of ideas without sacrificing any of the higher order thinking of more 'complex' texts. So in this book I follow Freire and try to consciously make sense of my experience in collaboration with the experiences of others and then express that learning in the way I know best as a way of understanding more about teacher education.

The dream job was turning into a nightmare. I just couldn't be myself. So how did other people manage in this key area of education? I got talking to people at conferences, on trains, in cafeterias and corridors. I wanted to tell that story. So I started with me and gathered some new ideas together.

REFERENCES

Anderson, L. (2006). Analytic autoethnography. *Journal of Contemporary Ethnography*, 35, 373–395.
Denzin, N. K. (2001). *Interpretive interactionism*. London: Sage.
Freire, P. (1972). *Pedagogy of the oppressed*. Harmondsworth: Penguin.
Hayler, M. (2003). *The writing cure? Writing, reflection and emotional development*, Unpublished EdD assignment, University of Brighton.
Kierkegaard, S. (1938). *The journals of Soren Kierkegaard*. Oxford: Oxford University Press.
Lewin, K. (1952). *Field theory in social science: Selected theoretical papers*. London: Tavistock.
Richardson, L. (2000). Writing: A method of inquiry. In N. K. Denzin, & Y. S. Lincoln (Eds.), *Handbook of qualitative research*, 923-948 London: Sage.
Sartre, J. -P. (1963). *The problem of method*. London: Methuen.

CHAPTER 2

INITIAL TEACHER EDUCATION AND AUTOETHNOGRAPHY

PRIMARY

I do remember my first day at Primary school which was in September 1964. My Mum and elder brother left me in the playground before school and I started crying as they walked away. I remember that my brother laughed and Mum smiled at my distress. She said there was nothing they could do and that it would be alright. She remembers being surprised at how upset I was because I was used to being at nursery all day. But the school was different from the nursery which was fairly small and new and wooden. The school was old and big and made from red brick and flint with a high wall and an iron gate. It was opened in 1870, had steps and corridors and windows that you couldn't see through. I worked there as an advisor forty years after that first day and, despite the excellent staff and all the efforts of planners and builders it still seemed to me like a place you might be sent as a punishment. I have an early memory from school of seeing the top of a bus going by above the wall and realising that 'real' life was continuing on the other side of the wall without me and that there was nothing I could do about it. That somewhat paradoxical feeling of being forgotten about and under the control of others, however nice they may be, seems to have been a source of anxiety for me throughout my time at school. After a few days in the infants I took a matchbox with somebody's dinner money in it and went into the shop on the way home to buy some sweets. My brother told my mother and she took me back to the school where the money was repaid and both parent and teacher disappointment was made clear to me. On his return from work that evening my father said he hoped I was ashamed of myself but I do not think I really was. The elements which stand out for me now when I consider this incident after years of study and work with children's emotional and behavioural difficulties are: the matchbox with an elastic band around it, which now seems like a strange way to bring your money to school; the fact that everybody walked home from school without their parents from the age of four onwards; and the complete lack of guilt on my part at being the first person ever in our family or either of my parents' families to have stolen something. I may well have pretended to feel sorry for my actions but as far as I remember I felt very little regret. Looking back I can see that my parents and teacher were concerned and that I liked that at some level since it meant that I was getting some attention. I was not popular at home that week but I was not forgotten. They were talking about me and talking to me.

I made friends in the infants and later in the junior part of the school. We played mainly war games and rough games like bulldog and piggy back fighting in the playground. My friend broke his teeth on the climbing frame and I began to learn

CHAPTER 2

how to read and write. It was slow going and there was some concern at my lack of effort and progress. I used to get *The Robin* and then *The Beano* comics but couldn't read many of the words by the time I went up to the juniors aged seven. I liked hearing the stories that my Mum and Dad read to me at bedtime such as *Brer Rabbit* and *Tarzan* but I don't remember bringing any books home from school or reading to them. My play became more imaginative and then collaborative around the age of seven and eight years old. I told my father about a game I was playing with model cowboys which involved the 'baddie' being dragged along the desert floor of our front room. Dad, a Quaker pacifist couldn't hide his sadness and disappointment at this sadistic streak in his youngest son. One of my best friends at this time was Sandra who lived next door. We played out many exciting games of adventure often based on the television programmes she had seen. She was three years older than me. I became the friend of Tim, a younger boy who lived down the road and we explored the neighborhood, local parks, woods and golf course where we became 'the two tornadoes': a couple not dissimilar to Batman and Robin and usually heavily armed. Some of these adventures of the imagination found their way into my school work as I began to learn how to write. Towards the end of my second year in junior school, when I was nine I managed to write a story called 'The Eskimo Singer' which was about a girl who grew up in the wild arctic and became a pop star. It was a bit like the day I painted the wooden thing at nursery school in that it stands out for me as a time when I was praised for being good and doing well, but it was not until my brother suggested that I must have copied the story that I realised that I had made something that impressed others. As well as a lesson in using and sharing imagination I may also have seen that I could get the attention of the people I cared about in positive ways by doing something good.

And I did care about that teacher. It was 1968 and she was the first teacher I had met who was too young to be my mother. I really wanted her positive attention and started to think about her all the time. She was also the first teacher I had who didn't hit me or anyone else. I soon got over the shock of being slapped on the legs or struck around the head by adults for the first time when I started school, but Miss Barcombe was one of the new generation of teachers: thoughtful, short-skirted and interested in the development of the whole child, she was the Plowden Report (1967) on stockingless legs and sandals. The school had made a good job of taking authoritarian post-war austerity well into the 1960s but the sun shone in and the Age of Aquarius began with her arrival. She must have found the head teacher of the school very strange indeed. Close to retirement, he often ended conversations with pupils by hitting them casually around the head. His hands were heavy and hard. Once, when my friend and I were being silly and noisy in class he appeared at the doorway and asked Miss Barcombe across the room whether she thought we should be sent permanently to 'the backward class' which silenced us with terror as intended and left Miss Barcombe opened-mouthed and unable to respond. The 'backward class' was only a step away from 'the backward school' and therefore 'the backward bus' which was sometimes called 'the spastic bus' but not often by me as my brother was on it. I would sometimes attack boys without explaining why when they shouted or laughed at the bus in the street. Not many people knew my brother went to the special school but it occurs to me now for the first time that my head teacher and Miss Barcombe probably did.

The imaginative games were getting a bit out of hand. My friend had some matches and we set fire to a shirt inside an old car we came across on some waste ground. We knocked on somebody's door to report the fire. When we got back to the car it was a blazing inferno and two fire engines came to put it out. We got some cautious credit for reporting the fire and Miss Barcombe got us to write about it when we were back in school. I felt guiltier about getting credit and being praised than I did about the car. I was uncomfortable with that sort of dishonesty, although not uncomfortable enough to make me confess and tell the truth.

My father took me away for two weekends. He had taken my brothers to Ireland and the West Country on cycling trips but I was too young to go so he and I went to the Isle of Wight and stayed in a youth hostel and on another weekend we walked and camped in Sussex. These trips may well have been a response to concerns that my parents had about my behaviour: "we thought that you might be feeling left out and it was your turn to have some time with Dad", says my mother. She remembers that there were some concerns about the boys I was playing with outside of school but not any real worries about my behaviour at that stage.

A LITERATURE REVIEW CONCERNING SUBJECT AND METHOD

In this chapter I consider the sometimes problematic relationship between the area of research and my method of researching it through discussion of some of the key research and literature in the areas where these activities, concepts and methodologies meet and overlap.

This review of research and writing is organised into two sections on Initial Teacher Education (ITE) and autoethnography respectively and seeks some working definitions and illustrations of the terms as I understand and use them in this book. My intention is to illustrate some of the philosophical and ideological influences upon the field and the method of my study, and then use these in interaction with each other to establish a working conceptual framework that forms the basis of the chapters that follow.

Inevitably, things get messy here and, as I was taught to do as a teacher, I attempt illumination, clarification and explanation through example and demonstration in a number of places.

Separating and Reuniting: Reviewing the Literature in Subject and Method

Bruner decried the creation of conceptual boundaries between thought, action and emotion followed by the construction of bridges to connect what should never have been separated (Bruner, 1986 p106). We need to examine the ways in which actions infuse our representations of the world. Activities and conceptions may

CHAPTER 2

need some degree of theoretical separation for examination and explanation but Bruner argues that they must remain connected and are made active and given meaning only in context with each other. It is the interaction and interdependence of these areas that Bruner considers as parts of the same whole (Bruner, 1986,1990).

While this review of literature discusses the phenomena of Initial Teacher Education and the concepts of autoethnography, memory, narrative and identity as particular areas of activity and methods of research, my aim is to consider closely the ways in which they relate to each other through teacher educators themselves and the points where the borders become permeable and begin to overlap. This involves the pairing and infusing of content and method in research through the self-narratives of those who are responsible for the initial education of teachers within university schools of education in England.

INITIAL TEACHER EDUCATION (ITE)

Lots of people are involved in the education of teachers. Learning to teach goes back a long way in the lives of those who teach. Our own education gives us a familiarity with the profession unlike any other. Lortie (1975) estimated that by the time a person begins a course of teacher education they have spent around thirteen thousand hours observing teachers. For those who choose to be teachers the partnerships between schools and schools of education or teacher training institutions have required students to work with a wide variety of people of all ages and from all walks of life (DfES, 2005). Education in and of education continues after qualification with an NQT year and then a whole career of Continuing Professional Development involving the gathering of experience and professional growth as careers and skills develop. This is a journey those who wish to teach set out upon and from which they are encouraged to continue until retirement. The process of learning and developing is required to never end and while some features remain consistent and grow at the core of practice, in education and in ITE change itself has been the centrally consistent feature of the last thirty years (DfEE, 1996; Bottery and Wright 2000; Burn, 2006).

The core study of this book takes place within the area of Initial Teacher Education (ITE) where abbreviations and acronyms proliferate (see list of acronyms) and which refers here to the undergraduate and post-graduate full-time and part-time courses that lead to Qualified Teacher Status (QTS), where students learn to be teachers while completing a degree such as the Bachelor of Education (BEd), Bachelor of Arts (BA with QTS), Bachelor of Science (BSc with QTS) or the Postgraduate Certificate in Education (PGCE). These are run by Higher Education Institutions (HEI) such as university schools of education in partnership with schools where students complete work-based placements.

All QTS courses are ratified and largely funded by the Training and Development Agency (TDA) and now referred to throughout all government literature as 'teacher training'. There are a growing number of Continuing Professional Development (CPD) courses that lead to QTS such as the School-Centred Initial Teacher Training

(SCITT) programme, the Graduate Teacher Programme (GTP) and the Registered Teacher Programme (RTP).

The education and training of teachers through university schools of education is an important area of the education system. It can be seen as the place where higher education and the education of children meet and where differing ideas and beliefs about the purposes of education come under intensive scrutiny and contest (see for example Bailey and Robson, 2002; Brisard et al., 2002; Furlong, 2005; Hartley, 2000; Richards et al., 1998; Winter, 2000).

In 2011, as positions are again being drawn, and the proposed re-structuring of the system for the preparation of teachers provokes fiscal and ideological arguments around the concepts of 'teacher training' and 'teacher education' the need to hear the voices of those who teach teachers is of key importance.

How Did We Get Here?

It is possible to see how things have changed in teacher education in England and Wales during the last 50 years by considering developments in education policy as a whole (see Appendix 1 for a chronology of selected major events in teacher education 1960–2010). The McNair Report of 1944 had condemned the existing arrangements for the 'recognition, training and the supply of teachers' as 'chaotic and ill-adjusted' to the needs of the nation (McNair,1944, p.18) and recommended the establishment of University led schools, institutes or centres of education for the local administration of the training of teachers. This had been adopted and developed in a number of guises and formats by 1960 through the Area Training Organisations (Dent, 1975). The 1950s saw a massive expansion of the permanent teacher training institutions fuelled by the Emergency Teacher Training Programme in response to a serious shortage of teachers (Lynch, 1979). The three-year teacher certificate course began in 1960 just a few months before Lord Robbins was appointed to review the pattern of full-time higher education and advise the government of the day on its principles and long-term development (Alexander et al., 1984). Published in 1963 the Robbins Report gave considerable attention to the education of teachers noting that the training colleges:

> ...feel themselves to be only doubtfully recognised as part of the system of higher education and yet to have attained standards of work and a characteristic ethos that justify their claim to an appropriate place in it (Robbins, 1963 p107).

From Robbins came an unprecedented expansion in the numbers of students studying to be teachers, a further rapid growth in the size and number of colleges and university departments now providing degree courses in education. The minimum length of undergraduate courses was increased to three years. In 1969 the first four-year BEd students graduated with QTS. Recognising the key role that ITE would play in the reform and restructuring of schools and pedagogical approaches, Plowden (1967) called for a full enquiry into teacher education. A

CHAPTER 2

select committee of 1970 reported widely differing approaches, curricula and standards of practice in teacher education and training around the country and the James Committee was appointed to investigate and report on the content and organisation of courses. The committee's report and proposals (DES, 1972b) demonstrate a view of teacher education as integrally linked with higher education. The need for teachers to be students and graduates of education as well as being trained and articled is central to the James Report recommendations of three cycles of teacher education linking a 2-year Diploma in Higher Education with 2 years of focused preparation for the teaching profession and a statutory CPD sabbatical term during each of the first seven years of service. Economic instability meant that few elements of the responding white paper, *Education: a framework for expansion* (DES, 1972a), came into place:

> For the teacher training institutions, the title of the white paper proved to be hollow – and the rhetoric of expansion was overtaken by the reality of contraction (Porter in Brock, 1996 p40).

Increasing emphasis on control of public expenditure by central government meant that while two areas of teacher education, the NQT year and the setting up of a statutory body to oversee ITE can be traced back to James, the absence and removal of key elements make the links remote. Succeeding administrations were to exercise unprecedented political control over education and the education of teachers in the 1980s and 90s (see Appendix 1). New Labour governments continued to demonstrate distrust for institutions concerned with the education of teachers through, for example, an increased emphasis on school-centred courses. England (England and Wales until the Welsh assembly took responsibility for education in Wales in 1999) led the way in these reforms which remain unparalleled elsewhere in Europe.

Despite some changes in the rhetoric of inspection Initial Teacher Education remains an area of intense scrutiny and tight control. The last 30 years has seen increasing political involvement in ITE as the changing face of education has had an increasingly direct effect upon ITE. This was accelerated in the 1990s with some of the most significant and challenging educational reforms of the decade taking place in ITE itself in the shape of the introduction of a statutory national curriculum for the training and education of teachers (DFEE, 1998) and continuing into the next decade with a revised ITE curriculum (DfES, 2005) and a new continuum of Professional Standards for Teachers in England at all stages of their education and careers (TDA 2007). Quality control structures and systems have been introduced to ensure the implementation of these policies and legislation as part of the effort to 'raise standards of achievement' in state schools through ensuring the 'competence', 'standard' and 'quality' of those who enter the teaching profession, defined by what Miller (2007) describes as a "tight, singular model of curriculum, of pedagogy and of assessment" (p.101).

The cultural transmission of both epistemology and pedagogy within these requirements made upon ITE has been highlighted over several curriculum areas

(Gilroy, 2002; Miller, 2007). DfEE Circular Number 4/98 stated the standards which all 'trainees' must achieve to be awarded QTS containing sections on 'Pedagogical knowledge and understanding required to secure pupils' progress', 'Effective teaching and assessment methods' and 'Trainees' knowledge and understanding' (DfEE, 1998 p66).

Alongside these requirements came the system of inspection and the criteria of the OFSTED quality assurance framework within which 'providers' of 'teacher training' continue to operate and under which it has been argued opportunities for alternative epistemologies, curricula or pedagogies are constrained in a way never before seen in UK universities (Miller, 1998, 2007; Ball, 2003). Miller (2007) uses Foucault's analytical tools and terms in a study of student experience and development, to illustrate how technologies of surveillance have developed in teacher education and how a discourse of 'training' and 'trainee' attempts to reduce and restrict the process of becoming teachers within 'technicist managerialism'.

Although the details are as yet unclear, the 2010 Education White Paper (DfE 2010) and comments from education ministers indicate that in the near future 'teacher training' will be based largely within schools, around a model of 'apprenticeship.' (e.g Minister of Education Michael Gove in *The Daily Telegraph*, 22 November, 2010)

WORKING IN ITE

As 'training' is used instead of 'education' throughout these documents and 'students' became 'trainees' in the late 1990s so the teacher educators were constructed here as 'teacher trainers' and schools of education became 'providers' of 'teacher training'. There has been some resistance to this nomenclature of re-branding from within the profession but it continues to represent and play its part in the reconstruction of power in teacher education away from the more autonomous situation in universities before 1998.

Accounts from the participants in my research presented in Chapter 5 confirm the significant influence upon the work of teacher educators of their own perceptions of what Ball sees as the dominant force of managerialism in higher education being exerted through:

> ...a technology, a culture and a mode of regulation that employs judgements, comparisons and displays as means of incentive, control, attrition and change – based on rewards and sanctions (both material and symbolic). The performances...serve as measures of productivity or output, or displays of 'quality'...(Ball, 2003 p.216).

It could be argued that like teachers, those working in teacher education were never very autonomous individually and that pressure has always been exerted by students, by institutions, by local authorities and by society as a whole (Bottery and Wright, 2000; Smetham and Adey, 2005). Indeed, as Maguire's (2000) examination of UK teacher education in the nineteenth century

CHAPTER 2

demonstrates state regulation of this area was not invented in the 1980s. However, the wide ranging changes arising from and driven by direct government involvement in the details of ITE in the late 20th century, particularly in the 1990s, meant that those tutors based in university schools of education faced a number of personal and professional dilemmas similar in some ways to those faced by teachers in primary and secondary schools following the 1988 Education Reform Act.

Peter Gilroy (Edwards et al., 2002) concluded that by 2001 his own professional life "consisted of negotiating a series of ambivalences – and indeed outright contradictions" (p1) between what he professed in his teaching and writing and his actual experience and practice within teacher education. He describes an academic life where he needed to accommodate the fact that teacher education was being fixed into apparent certainties along with his work on the contingent and shifting nature of knowledge in professionalism and teacher education. Such sensations of dissonance arise in all professions in times of change but are rarely as apparent as they can be in teacher education where the articulation of beliefs about teaching and learning is a central feature of the job.

Korthagen, Loughran, and Lunenberg (2005) illustrate that as well as supporting student teachers' learning about teaching, teacher educators also model the role of the teacher through their own teaching. This is a point developed by Lunenberg, Korthagen, and Swennen (2007):

> In this respect, the teacher education profession is unique, differing from, say, doctors who teach medicine. During their teaching, doctors do not serve as role models for the actual practice of the profession i.e., they do not treat their students. Teacher educators, conversely, whether intentionally or not, teach their students as well as teach about teaching (p588).

Tillema and Kremer-Hayon (2005) examine the dilemmas faced by teacher educators in complying with external standards on the one hand while trying to maintain and develop the pedagogy of teacher education on the other. As my experience and my data for this research confirms, belief can come head to head with practice in such a situation where the 'dilemmas constitute a powerful means of ascertaining a professional's perspectives on action' (Windschtl, 2002 p132). Lunenberg, Korthagen, and Swennen (2007) examine if and how teacher educators model new visions of learning in their own practice and concur with Putnam and Borko (1997) that while the 'notion that students of teaching should be treated as active learners who construct their own understandings' (p587) has become almost a mantra in teacher education, the reality of practices in teacher education is much more complex.

This is an analysis that has also led to doubts about the extent of the influence that teacher education has upon the practice of students once they become teachers. Having analysed the effectiveness of teacher education from a more general angle, Wideen, Mayer-Smith, and Moon (1998) conclude that the impact of teacher education on practice seems to be unclear, due largely to a significant absence from the existing research:

> One aspect that appeared to be missing from the research was the teacher educators themselves. We found very few studies that thoughtfully examined the work of the university education professor (pp.169–170).

It appears that not much had changed in this area since Howey and Zimpher (1990) noted that very little is known about the characteristics of teacher educators even though they are perceived to be responsible for the quality of teachers. Lanier and Little (1986) note that:

> ...teachers of teachers—what they are like, what they do, what they think—are systematically overlooked in studies of teacher education. Even researchers are not exactly sure of who they are (p528).

It seems that those who have been most involved in teacher education have themselves been least prominent during what has been a period of radical change: "we hear the voices of university researchers" wrote Fenstermacher in 1997, "of law makers, and of policy analysts about what teacher educators do or fail to do, but we do not often hear the voices of teacher educators" (Fenstermacher in Loughran and Russell, 1997 p3). Edited volumes from Russell and Munby (1992), Loughran and Russell (1997), and Brock (1996) give space for these voices from an international perspective. Britzman (1991) makes a critical study of learning to teach in the USA and uses narratives of students to examine the 'structure of experience and the experience of structure' within school placement work in particular. Furlong and Smith (1996) and Furlong (2000) consider the professional education of teachers in the UK from the perspective of students in ITE. The distinctive contribution of higher education as a partner in this professional preparation forms the framework of studies by Burn (2006), Ellis (2007) and Morrison and Pitfield (2006) as they focus upon the implications of developing pedagogy, and subject knowledge for practice.

While life-history approaches have been widely and productively employed in researching student, beginning and senior teachers' lives (e.g. Bullough, 1989; Bullough et al., 1992; Cohen, 1991; Goodson, 2003) and have often examined central issues such as gender, race and class in relation to education, culture and identity through this lens (e.g. Basit, 1997; Merrill, 1999; Osler, 1997; Weber, 1998) they have rarely been employed to examine the lives of teacher educators. Ball and Goodson (1985) advocate life history research methods in education because they can highlight the political and ideological climates in which teachers' lives are embedded. For Antikainen et al (1996) the subjective life history located within context holds the key perspective 'through which, and also in which, the social finds expression' (p17).

If as argued throughout this book, identity and pedagogy are constructed through a self-narrative of lived experience within all its historical, social and cultural contexts, it follows that the experiences of teacher educators offer insight and illumination in this key area of education.

CHAPTER 2

Teacher educators can sometimes be heard reflecting upon their careers in schools within the research and writing about the professional lives of school teachers (Goodson, 1988, 1992, 2003; Hargreaves, 1998; Sikes et al., 1985) but these studies do not follow the story through to examine participants' work in ITE, the focus being upon their former careers in schools. Noel (2006) does examine the experiences of those new to working in teacher education in the learning and skills sector, while Murray (2005) and Murray and Male (2005) also draw on evidence from novice teacher educators themselves when considering the process of induction into higher education.

SELF-STUDY IN TEACHER EDUCATION

From 1986 Clandinin and Connelly have highlighted the use of narrative and story in the education of teachers in Canada. Drawing from both Polkinghorne's psychological research (1988) and from the philosophical ideas of Paul Ricoeur (1984, 1985, 1988) Connelly and Clandinnin (1990) developed their research to demonstrate how practitioners' narrative ways of knowing become the primary form by which they make meaning of their experiences. This body of research shows how teachers use and construct knowledge that is experiential, narrative and relational, and how this shapes and is further shaped by, the contexts of their professional lives (e.g. Clandinin and Connelly, 1986, 1987, 1991, 1995, 1999; Connelly and Clandinin, 1988, 1990, 2001; Connelly). The role of narrative is central:

> Narrative for us is the study of how humans make meaning of experience by endlessly telling and retelling stories about themselves that both refigure the past and create purpose in the future. Deliberately storying and restorying one's life or a group or cultural story is, therefore a fundamental method of personal and social growth: it is the fundamental quality of education (Connelly and Clandinin, 1990, p24).

The focus upon the use of students' and tutors' own narratives of experience and self-study in order to make meaning of that experience relevant to themselves as teachers and teacher educators led to the formation of the Self Study of Teacher Education Practices (S-STEP) special interest group in 1993. The focus here has been largely upon the use of narrative to support the education and professional development of teachers through reflective self-study (Russell and Munby, 1992: Russell and Loughran, 2007). The narrative approach makes transparent and active the ways in which a personal/professional past is linked to a personal/professional future for students preparing to be teachers. Clandinin sees this as a particular kind of knowledge:

> We see personal, practical knowledge as in the person's past experience, in the person's present mind and body and in the person's future plans and actions (Clandinin in Russell and Munby 1992, p125).

Recent research using S-STEP methodology has included seeking to develop practice by placing teacher educators' own narratives at the centre of the process in order to examine the role of collaboration in self-study (Chryst et al., 2008: Crafton and Smolin, 2008) and exploring the tensions between teaching, methodology and theory in ITE (Hamilton, 2008). Kitchen's (2008) study of his own experiences of moving from school teaching towards tenure as a university professor reveals the struggle of balancing teaching and scholarship for teacher educators which was a prominent issue for the participants of my own research as discussed in Chapter 5. These lines of research argue for recognition of alternative theories of knowledge including relational, narrative, and embodied ways of knowing and stress that teacher development policies and practices should recognise and support teachers' and teacher educators' inquiries into practice.

While my approach has been strongly influenced by the ways in which the methods used in the S-STEP special interest group bring narrative inquiry together with teacher education, my central aim is not as theirs is to directly investigate and change methodology within the practice of teacher education (Heston et al., 2008, p10). My aim is rather to develop an understanding of how the professional identity of teacher educators is both formed and represented by narratives of experience. Clearly this has implications for practice and policy informing my work as a teacher educator and educational researcher. I also wanted to contribute towards professional knowledge by using a method of sharing and gathering responses to my own auto-biographical writing as a way of exploring how professional lives develop. Like Clandinnin (in Russell and Munby, 1992, p125) I have come to believe that our personal, practical knowledge lays in our past experience, present mind, future plans and actions.

To bring these elements of past and present together in order to illuminate and understand belief and practice in ITE, I needed to choose and develop methods of autoethnographic research.

MAKING MEMORY METHODOLOGY

> Memory…produces at the opportune moment a break which also inaugurates something new. It is the strangeness, the alien dynamic, of memory which gives it the power to transgress the law and the local space in question; from out of the unfathomable and ever-shifting secrets, there comes a sudden 'strike'…details, intense singularities, which already function in memory as they do when circumstances give them an opportunity to intervene: the same timing in both occasions, the same artful relation between the concrete detail and the conjecture, the latter figuring alternatively as the trace of a past event, or as the production of some new harmony (de Certeau, 1980 p41–42).

How the 'artful relation' between detail and conjecture inaugurates new harmonies of understanding in ITE will be demonstrated and examined in Chapter 5. In this section of Chapter 2, I discuss memory, autoethnography and finally analytic autoethnography as a methodology in the context of narratives of learning, and

CHAPTER 2

explain my reasons for selecting some of the powerful if unwieldy tools from this particular research toolbox.

Memory and the Self

Memory and the past should here be immediately distinguished from nostalgia which as Dennis Potter said in a BBC interview in 1991:

> ...puts things safely in the past. What I say and what I know we do with our own lives is we know that the past is suddenly standing smack in front of us, not behind us and we know that it can infiltrate into the very future or the present in ways that don't permit nostalgia. Nostalgia says 'oh those dear dead days, those golden days oh how I felt on x day' – which is safely putting it back. Whereas if it's jogging alongside you, and nodding at you and grinning at you and pulling at you and then suddenly standing and gibbering in front of you then you know that you are one piece with what you have been and what you will be. That doesn't permit nostalgia (BBC, 1991).

Whereas Kundera (2002, p.5) defines nostalgia more bleakly as 'the suffering caused by an unappeased yearning to return', Potter famously uses elements of nostalgia as a way of beginning this dialogue with the past in his plays, although he never leaves it there:

> You can use nostalgia to suddenly hit. I would sometimes seek to use a cheap little song to suddenly go 'wham' with what was actually being felt which is always more complicated than that. But the song gives you the access to it, it strips away something and stings and then you realise what it was you were feeling (BBC, 1991).

Potter's description of his intention and technique illuminates both the power and the seemingly arbitrary nature of memory. While we may seek to understand ourselves and others through the past by knowing that we are 'one piece' with what we 'have been' the power of memory comes not from precision or accuracy but from how we relate to our constructions and re-constructions of the past as we are now. Eliot identified the working of unconscious selection in the process when he asked:

> Why, for all of us, out of all we have heard, seen, felt in a lifetime do certain images recur, charged with emotion, rather than others?...such memories may have symbolic value but of what we cannot tell, for they come to represent the depths of feeling into which we cannot peer (Eliot, 1933 p148).

Peering into those depths to extract meaning and to examine the process itself has become more popular and possible than it seemed to Eliot although some of his literary peers were exploring this in his day: Woolf begins *The Waves* (1943) with a series of what Craig Raine (2008 p.22) describes as 'ordinary epiphanies' and Joyce opened a new era for the novel with an anthology of almost subliminal memories like snapshots in *Portrait of the Artist as a Young Man* (1916). Nabakov who argued that the true purpose of autobiography is to follow thematic designs through ones life (1951) evoked the past through what Field (1977) calls 'puppets of memory' such as his own teachers who became characters in his books. Deploying the fictional with the factual in retelling differing versions to create the ever-shifting text of his autobiography Nabakov suggested that the 'reality' of a life retold cannot be possessed by 'the esteemed visitor' of the reader and is continually revised and recreated by its author. This suggestion of a recursive dialogue between the 'core' and the situated self as between the self as individual and the self within a community resonates throughout this book.

My own research technique and intention has been to construct and then to share my own story with other teacher educators as a way of gaining access and new understandings of our experiences, beliefs and practice. Our discussions and writing revealed the ways in which we gain 'access' to memory and how that makes us who we think we are.

Rousseau recognised the possibilities and the limitations of using only memory as he addressed the purpose of education in his *Confessions* of 1781:

> I have only one faithful guide on which I can count; the succession of feelings which have marked the development of my being…I may omit or transpose facts, or make mistakes in dates; but I cannot go wrong about what I have felt, or about what my feelings have led me to do; and these are the chief subjects of my story. (Rousseau, 1781/1953 p262).

Rosen develops the concept of 'making memory' from Stephen Rose (1992) and the role of social memory from Fentress and Wickham (1992) through his own stories of childhood (Rosen 1993) and the wider study of autobiographical discourse (Rosen 1998).

I might here attempt to make another distinction between memories of personal experience as the focus of this research and memories of personal experience as a lens through which to view the subject of teacher education. It can be argued that while autoethnography draws upon autobiography as a genre of writing and research it is not autobiography; it is not 'about' the researcher or writer as such. From this perspective this research is not *about* me or the other participants. The variety of approaches that have personal experiences at the centre may look at a range of issues and phenomena through the lens of life experience but by using these methods researchers and writers such as me also indicate that those experiences, those lives whether they are our own or the lives of others, or a combination of both, do, to a certain and central extent, make the phenomena. After all what else is there but memory? Being forced, to return to Kierkegaard's image (1938), to live our lives forwards we seek understanding through memory. Seen from this perspective what else are we other than our history and what else is teacher education in universities other than the experiences of teacher educators and the people they work with? How else could you look at this and begin to know what it is like?

Auto/biographical, life-history and narrative methodologies have moved from the margins to become established, although not unchallenged, within educational research. Pioneering studies with teachers in various contexts by for example Ball

CHAPTER 2

and Goodson (1985), Elbaz (1990), Huberman (1993) and Erben (1998) among others form a rigorous and widely-respected foundation in demonstrating the valuable insights that are gained into teachers, students, schools and pedagogy through the examination of participants' life-histories. Through her longitudinal study of primary school teachers Nias (1989) demonstrates that practitioners' lives are not easily separated from their craft, making the now well-established argument that 'the self is a crucial element in the way teachers themselves construct the nature of their job' (Nias, 1989 p13).

West et al., (2007) argue that by questioning the ways in which we conceptualise knowledge and learning, educational research approaches which focus upon the auto/biographical challenge both policy and practice in education as they foreground notions of agency and the making of meaning from experience in opposition to deterministic instrumentalism:

> In education, biographical research has combined with more humanistic ways of theorising learning, education and pedagogical practices, focussing for instance on personal development and growth (West et al., 2007 p12).

The various approaches that come under the auto/biographical, life-history and narrative banners commonly challenge forms of research which marginalise and abstract the perspectives of participants. Life history approaches have been used to illuminate relationships between learning, identity and race (Basit, 1997), class (Merrill, 1999) and gender (Weber, 1998). They have been employed to examine learning in traditional and alternative settings and in studies of learning and professional identity (Brookfield, 1995; West, 1996). While each of these studies carries a different emphasis and preoccupation and draw upon a range of various intellectual sources they hold in common an interest in the participant as person. As an investigation of teacher educators' identity and their perceptions of their work this book shares in that tradition.

Brookfield (1995) links the lens of autobiography with the skills of becoming a reflective teacher by making the individual's role in the shaping of professional identity and the phenomena of education a central focus. The biographical perspective clarifies the understanding of learning and teaching with a view to empowerment rather than measurement. Learning is re-conceived as a subjective process realised in specific historical and cultural contexts. Weber and Mitchell (1995) and Mitchell and Weber (1999) invite teachers to use a variety of life-history informed methods to revisit their past, their attitudes and their beliefs so that they can examine and reinvent themselves as teachers. From this perspective teachers are agents in the building of knowledge and the development of pedagogy, however prescribed it may have become:

> ...they are once more both creators in, as well as created by, the social and cultural worlds they inhabit (West et al., 2007 p32)

The processes in which we construct memory and the ways in which it informs practice are central themes here and therefore I and the other participants are part of both the topic and the method of research. Our narratives become both method

18

and data that is empirically derived from our own articulated experience and observation.

Autoethnography: Self-culture Research

Autoethnography has increasingly become the term of choice for a range of methods of research, analysis and writing that employ personal experience as a way of investigating and understanding the sub-cultures and the wider cultures of the societies we live and work within. I imagine autoethnography as a toolbox within the qualitative research workshop. In common these methods and research tools focus upon the memories of events, feelings, thoughts and emotions which contribute through varying methods of recall, collection and analysis towards different types of systematic introspection in order to illuminate and to facilitate understanding.

Debates continue about where the toolbox sits and what that systematic introspection should entail. The current discourse of the genre refers almost exclusively to what Anderson (2006) critiques as 'evocative autoethnography' which draws upon postmodern sensibilities and rejects realist and analytic ethnographic traditions. Anderson proposes the term 'Analytic Autoethnography' as a way of reframing and reclaiming autoethnography within what he terms 'the analytic ethnographic paradigm.' His intention is to re-open and develop a research approach in which the researcher is deeply self-identified as a member while maintaining the qualitative principles of traditional symbolic interactionism.

Hayano (1979), who coined the term 'autoethnography', used it to refer to the work of 'insider' anthropologists, researching their 'own people' (p101) arguing that in a post- colonial era ethnographers need to study their own social worlds and sub-cultures. It has evolved and widened from there to include a sometimes bewildering rubric of research approaches, methods and techniques such as 'narratives of the self' (Richardson 1994), 'personal experience narratives' (Denzin 1989), 'first person accounts'(Ellis 1998), 'reflective ethnographies' (Ellis and Bochner 1996), 'evocative narratives' (Tillman-Healy 1999), 'collaborative autobiography' (Goldman, 1993) and, as applied to teacher education by Clandinin and Connelly (1994), 'personal experience methods', to name only a few (see Denzin and Lincoln, 2000 for a comprehensive summary and Anderson et al., 2006 for a critical debate). Within all of these approaches the researcher is deeply self-identified through explicit and reflective self-observation.

Bochner (in Ellis and Bochner, 2000) describes a variation of emphasis among autoethnographers as they move along what he calls three axes of the self (auto), culture (ethnos) and descriptive research (graphy) adopting one and/or other of these many available terms and tools within the autoethnographic approach. My approach has been to use a number of research methods that come from this particular toolbox and to which several of these sub-categories can be applied, because I wanted to examine some of the commonalities that arise in the experiences of teacher educators while recognising the individual nature of experience. I wanted to examine and construct my own story towards and within

CHAPTER 2

ITE in collaboration with and reference to others. I also wanted to experiment with and attempt to introduce more reciprocity within the process of the research itself for reasons identified above concerning authenticity and identity. As the study developed and I continued to examine the various tributaries which feed into the autoethnographic stream, I was drawn towards Anderson's (2006) concept of analytic autoethnography as a framework within which to examine and present my research.

Using Autoethnography

I describe and explain the phases and strategies of the research in detail and in context within Chapter 3. In this chapter they provide a framework for the narrative story of the research as a way of exploring my reasons for using them.

I began the research by writing a self-narrative of my own memories of learning; a process Bochner describes as using one's own experience to examine a culture or sub-culture where the author deploys their own experiences to 'bend back on the self and look more deeply at the self-other interactions' (Ellis and Bochner, 2000, p740). Here the researcher's own memories of experience illuminate and allow access to the sub-culture under study; in my case the sub-culture of teacher educators.

Anderson (2006) also sees full membership in the research group or setting as a key element of analytic autoethnography. Sharing the self-narrative with six people who work as teacher educators in university schools of education was the way in which I attempted to situate and contextualise the narrative alongside others. I wanted to draw out some commonalities as well as stimulate contrary perspectives. Ellis and Bochner describe a similar process of 'reflective ethnography' starting research from ones own experience, developing to ethnographies 'where the researcher's experience is studied along with other participants' (Ellis and Bochner in Denzin and Lincoln, 2000 p. 740). Anderson (2006) agrees that because of its direct and unfettered character, self-narrative can be used to develop and refine understandings of social processes and situations while taking the reader to the depths of personal feeling in a way that no other research method can, but he warns against self-absorbed digression and insists on the 'ethnographic imperative of dialogic engagement with others in the social worlds we seek to understand' (p 385).

While my own story forms a central part of the investigation because that is the story of teacher education that I think I know best, I was always keen to engage the voices of others as a way of questioning and developing that understanding and to share and compare experiences so as to extend that understanding further. Our relational narratives are both method and data that acknowledge Atkinson, Coffey and Delamont's warning that:

> We must not lose sight of the ethnographic imperative that we are seeking to understand and make sense of complex social worlds of which we are only part (but a part nevertheless) (2003, p57).

Distinctions between the personal and the cultural are easily and deliberately blurred by such a process. Indeed the blurring seems to me to be a central aspect of the relationship between the individual and the culture which they contribute towards as they are shaped by it. Ethnographic reflexivity itself is, as Davies (1999) observes, most appropriately seen as a relational rather than a purely subjective activity where 'interrelationships between the researcher and other inform and change social knowledge' (Davies, 1999 p184). Following the principles of analytic rather than evocative autoethnography in this aspect of my research, my method was grounded in self-experience but reaches beyond it as well.

Autoethnography as a method of research has been seen as both the toolbox and a tool within the box. Van Maanen (1988) sees it as a sub-method of 'impressionistic accounts', while Tedlock (1991) refers to it as part of 'narrative ethnography'. Denzin (1997) includes autoethnography as a sub-category of 'interpretive ethnography'. In 1996 it was still part of the 'new or experimental ethnography' for Ellis and Bochner but they champion it as the wider generic term for the 'post-modern ethnographic approaches' of Tyler (1986) and others by 2000 (Denzin and Lincoln, 2000). Anderson (2006) links it closely to a stream of work flowing from the 1920s Chicago School that have continued to incorporate aspects of self-related study into analytic ethnographic practice.

A collection of connected methodological strategies has also been developed as autoethnographic projects have been used more widely in anthropology, education, sociology and communication studies. The proliferation of terms, methods and strategies represent the post-structural splintering of qualitative research approaches and definitions in what Lincoln and Denzin describe as the 'seventh moment' of qualitative research (Lincoln and Denzin, 2000). Lincoln and Denzin (2000) led the call for a wholehearted move into this seventh phase where a 'broad, interpretive, post-experimental, post-modern, feminist and critical sensibility' (p.1050) can find its place alongside the positivist, post-positivist, humanistic and naturalistic conceptions and analysis of human experience. They offer no easy solutions for resolving the tensions within this paradigm, but counsel acceptance and transparency in dealing with the crises of representation and legitimacy.

Smith and Deemer (2000) attempt to move the discussion on from the unproductive arguments about paradigms and the site of dispute may have shifted in recent years. Flyvbjerg (2001) calls on all social scientists to stop competing on self-defeating terms and to embrace different but equally valid forms of rigorous research. In fact, as Lincoln and Denzin make clear, we have little choice:

> It is not that we might elect to engage in work that is postmodern. Rather, it is that we have inherited a postmodern world, and there is no going back. We do not 'choose' to be postmodern. The historical moment has chosen us. (Lincoln and Denzin, 2000, p1060).

Within this 'moment' the researcher can find or create a new tool of use for each of the elements and methods of their research and writing. Qualitative researchers draw on experience to assemble the *'bricolage'* envisioned by Levi-Strauss (1966) where context is everything and the *bricoleur,* 'a Jack of all trades or a kind of

21

CHAPTER 2

professional do-it-yourself person' (ibid p.17), produces an emergent construction that takes on new forms as new tools and materials are added to the picture. Central for the bricoleur is an understanding of the interactive nature of the research process and how this is shaped by their personal history and those of the people they work with in making a complex, reflexive, collage-like creation that represents the researcher's images understandings, and interpretations of the phenomenon under analysis (Weinstein and Weinstein, 1991 p.164).

Although there are many epistemological questions beneath it I think that autoethnography may be the toolbox of the bricoleur precisely because of its loose and changing application. As Ellis points out:

> Perhaps the loose application of the term autoethnography only signifies a greater tolerance now for the diverse goals of ethnography and a better understanding of the fallibility and indeterminacy of language concepts (Ellis and Bochner, 2000 p.743).

Definition becomes more difficult within this loose application which aims to objectify the subjective to an extent through reflexivity. My aim here is to explain and demonstrate my method so perhaps I need to open the toolbox and choose a different way. If splintering definitions or fragmenting codes of language will no longer do and personal experience is at the centre of this literature of method then a moment of reflection is called for where the process might be made more transparent through a different voice. I wrote the following section as I wrestled with these ideas and the competing definitions of autoethnography.

REFLECTION

As the text slips away from me I read through what I've written again and start to think about how I would assess it and respond to it as a tutor if someone had sent it to me. Why? Is that what this is all about? Am I trying to write for an external set of standards and in a particular way? I could take the writing above and chisel and shape it and make it more and more like the chapters and the articles and the books I've been reading for the last year and less and less like me. *Less and less like me.* Some of the books and the notes I've written are lying around me on the floor and on my desk. I want to breathe them all in and then breathe them out and onto the page as my own. I reach down and pick up something I copied from Maria Antoniou's (2002) thesis a month ago:

> 'We need to support each other in rejecting the limitations of a tradition – a manner of reading of speaking, of writing, of criticizing – which was never really designed to include us at all.' (Rich, 1987, 1981, p.95)

My scribbled note is squashed against the quote: 'we?' 'us?'

Then my notes paraphrase Maria as she writes of how 'this disturbs the myth of the objective academic' (p39) and how she took a new turn on her literature chapter from there, how she made a new approach, made a new beginning that was open about the partiality of her reading, that got down to what mattered in her thesis and stopped pretending to be 'complete' or 'objective'.

I look up from my notes. Across the room I can see my reflection in the computer screen. The words I've typed cover my face like a mask. *Less and less like me.* I think I'd better take a new turn here. I may not be able to be wholly part of the 'we' and 'us' that Rich refers to and Antoniou identifies with but I don't seem to be able to join the tradition they both reject without wearing a mask of words and I'm not sure I've got the skills or the motivation to make one that fits. That's not why I'm doing this. Just the opposite if I remember rightly. This is my attempt to make connections between my past and my future, to understand how identities shift and are used in belief and in practice, and to find my way back to a sense of myself.

I gather up all the notes and put them on the desk. Put the books and the articles in a pile in the corner. That gives me some space. The floor is clear. On the shelves around the room are so many books, all sorts of books that have led me here. There's a story here somewhere:

Lots of stories in fact but what use are they to me now? How can they be part of this story? What sort of story is this? Maybe it's a mystery, a detective story. I go to the shelf and find some old Raymond Chandler books hidden behind a picture of my eldest son. Stories of how the dark 'truth' of human beings emerges the more you look beyond the surface. Left along the shelf I can see the collection of stories by Raymond Carver *Where I'm Calling From* (1993). One of the stories inside has that title. The narrator in that story knows it is time to be honest as he prepares to telephone his wife from the drying out clinic:

'She'll ask me where I'm calling from, and I'll have to tell her.' (p242)

That's what I want to do now with the rest of this chapter: tell you where I'm calling from amongst all these words.

Towards Analytic Autoethnography

Carver made art that left space for the reader to make meaning from the routine and the problematic moments in his characters lives. I think that qualitative sociological research must allow space for the *bricolage* of meaning and the in-depth understanding of the phenomenon in question. I agree with Denzin and Lincoln (2000) that there can be no clear window into the life of another. We are seldom able to give explanations even if the story we tell is our own.

At some point during my EdD study I moved into the uncertain, messy, multi-voiced, multi-texted world or worlds of the qualitative interpretist paradigm. I'd been heading that way for a while. For my first piece of 'independent research' as a 'mature' undergraduate I chose to research and write *A Publishing History of QueenSpark Books* (Hayler, 1989) the community writing and publishing group I became part of in 1988. I traced the history of the group as it emerged from local campaigns and handmade leaflets into a publishing collective making books of local stories and autobiographies which illuminated a history of Brighton constructed from the memories of working people. It was not so much that these stories from memories contradicted the 'official' history of the town but rather that the stories were transformed by being told from a different perspective. It wasn't that the stories of working experience were more 'true' than the stories about the powerful and famous of Brighton's past but they found an audience who related to them directly as stories about their town and about them. Nostalgia played its part inside this mix of what Stephen Yeo describes as a 'critique of Now running through a channel of Then' (Yeo, 1988, p46).

For me the foundations of certainties about the past and the self were being undone. My own story started to change as I looked back and followed Yeo to QueenSpark. He had moved on but there was another trail to follow. The trail went *out* into the town and beyond to the other groups that formed the Federation of Worker Writers and Community Publishers (the Fed), *in* as I reconnected with my past and made links to the idea of being a teacher and an academic of sorts in some sort of congruent identity, *back* into other stories of the past and the ways they are formed and used, and then *forward* as I researched and wrote about the Fed and the power of memory and prepared to prepare to be a teacher.

I read two books that had a particular impact on me at this time.

In his groundbreaking book *In Search of a Past* (1984) Ronald Fraser manages to combine his own recollections with the testimony and collected interviews of many others who knew him as a child to produce a many-voiced autobiography as a way of becoming the historian of his own past while gaining insight to his present self. Drawing upon sometimes competing methods of constructing past and self through oral history and psychoanalysis, Fraser weaves a series of encounters together to create a fragmented, reflective, reflexive narrative where no simple unified self emerges. Contradictory meanings are not resolved as Fraser acknowledges that: 'the difficulty of writing about the past...is part and parcel of the past' (p104) and that the past is a collective as well as an individual experience. Carolyn Steedman makes sense of her own childhood as she reflects upon her mother's life in *Landscape for a Good Woman* (1986), questioning whether the intellectual constructs she learned at university can adequately make sense of real lives and feelings and demonstrating that imagination, self-reflection and emotion are the critical if repressed faculties in the project of social theory. These books reconnect the authors with their own past as a way of understanding themselves after the long journey away from home that we know as education. Here perspectives are often defined by tensions, contradictions and hesitations which are acknowledged, as they often are in autoethnographic studies, as key aspects of the research. There is no attempt to 'iron out' the confusions or contradictions which stand, as they do within this approach, as key elements of our experience.

I have wanted to go back more than once. To step out of the mess onto a more certain, steady, at least near-positivist world where I might remove myself from the research or at least disguise myself in the text. But the more I have tried to do that the less and less it seems like me and the more I have realised that writing is always a story of the self in one way or another.

Some stories can stand alone and allow readers to make their own analysis to a certain extent. Here I need to share my methods of analysis and share the ways in which these stories can be viewed.

Analytic Authoethnography

Anderson (2006) makes the case for Analytic Autoethnography rather than what he calls 'evocative autoethnography.' Writing with research students who may be contending with the pull of various approaches to qualitative inquiry partly in mind, Anderson argues that there has always been an autoethnographic element in qualitative social research citing classic studies from Chicago School ethnography such as Nels Anderson's *The Hobo* (1923), Roth's *Timetables* (1963) and Davis's study of *The Cabdriver and His Fare* (1959). However these authors did not explicitly identify themselves as reflective self-observers in the style of contemporary autoethnographers. Deegan (2001) agrees that the Chicago school students often lived and worked in the settings they studied while acknowledging that the self is not the primary source or focus within these studies in the ways suggested and demonstrated by more recent evocative autoethnographers such Ellis and Bochner (2000, 2006).

Anderson (2006) proposes three key principles that inform the five distinct features of analytic autoethnography. These provide a framework that came to suit my purpose for this research study and offered me a way forward in meeting the requirements of the thesis. Anderson marks autoethnography as a distinct subgenre within the broader practice of analytical ethnography.

Put most simply, analytical autoethnography refers to the ethnographic work in which the researcher is (a) a full member in the research group or setting (b) visible as such a member in the researcher's published text and (c) committed to an analytical research agenda focussed on improving theoretical understanding (p375).

Denzin (2006) and Ellis and Bochner (2006) oppose such a structure arguing that it simply returns to a positivist research agenda leading towards the negation of the post-structural, anti-foundational elements which they see as central in autoethnography.

Building upon the key principles, Anderson proposes five features for an analytic autoethnography that is grounded in self-experience while reaching beyond it as well:

- Complete member research
- Analytical reflexivity
- Narrative visibility of the researcher's self
- Dialogue with informants beyond the self
- Commitment to theoretical analysis

Anderson (2006 p378)

This is the methodological framework I adopted and adapted for my own research.

CHAPTER 2

Chapter 3 describes how I applied and tested this approach through a description of the conduct of the research.

Making Meaning from Stories of Experience

How can the data gathered by the inevitably messy personal experience methods of autoethnography be analysed in an attempt to bring news of one world to another? While Denzin has stated that there is only interpretation in social science and criticises both Goffman (1959) and Garfinkel (1967) for attempting to extract abstract generalisations from auto/biographical data, he recommends Sartre's (1963) progressive/ regressive method of analysis which he reframes as 'critical interpretive method' (Denzin 2001 p.41).

The concept of the individual, defined as a praxis that both produces and is produced by social structures (Sartre, 1982) forms the basis of the progressive/regressive method as it combines psychological and sociological explanations of human action.

Here narrative is located in a particular historical situation. Sartre (1963) structured an analysis that first looks forward from a particular point towards a conclusion of sorts as well as back to the historical, cultural and biographical conditions that moved the narrator. This situates the memory and interpretation of actions in time and space, illuminating the uniqueness of the individual while revealing commonalities of the sub-culture.

The narrative analysis and organisation of Chapter 5 draws on the ideas of Sartre's method of analysis and pursues what Denzin (1997) calls the 'conjunctural, contextual, performance-based, "messy" approach to reading (and writing)' (p246). This is clearly not an approach that attempts to capture the totality of an individual or a group's way of life. The focus here is upon:

> ...interpreted slices, glimpses and specimens of interaction that display how cultural practices, connected to structural formations and narrative texts, are experienced at a particular time and place by interacting individuals (ibid p247).

In Chapter 5 I have strategically selected sites for interpretation and presentation that constitute points at which the narrative texts of our stories intersect and interact. This is a model that works upward and outward from the individual self-narratives gathered through writing and through interviews, towards the larger set of meanings that operate in the particular context of teacher education within university schools of education, offering a picture of what Fiske (1994 p195) describes as 'culture in practice' within ITE by placing one set of experiences and perspectives alongside others.

Employing a version of Sartre's (1963) progressive/regressive method of analysis allowed me to remain within the framework of analytic autoethnography without turning the stories told by me and the other participants into merely stories analysed and sacrificing meaning for particular notions of analytic rigor. These ethnographies are empirical in the classical sense of the word as they are based upon the articulated experiences of the participants in real and particular situations and places (Denzin, 1997). While not known as an ethnographer Sartre (1963, pp85–166) constructs a method that emphasises memories and the consequences of particular decisions and actions by looking first forward to the conclusion of a set of acts and then working back through the 'subjects'' interpretations of the conditions and situations that shaped the decisions and actions in question. In his famous biography of Flaubert, for example, Sartre (1993) uses this method to demonstrate how individuals internalise and express social events and values by illuminating those structures, firstly from the lived perspective of Flaubert (from his private and published writing) and then by investigating and describing the relevant social structures such as class, family and era themselves.

> The problem is to recover the totalising movement of enrichment which engenders each moment in terms of the prior moment, the impulse which starts from lived obscurities in order to arrive at the final objectification (Sartre, 1963 p147).

This forwards and backwards movement in time (see Appendix 2), characteristic of oral history and life history interviews and writing (e.g. Thompson, 1978; Goodson, 1992; Thomson, 1994) locates the participants and their actions ('subjects' and their 'projects' in Sartre's terms) within culture as a set of interpretive practices. The uniqueness of participants' experience is illuminated in the episodes revealed alongside similarities and commonalities with others. In this book my own memories of being threatened with the 'special class' by my head teacher when I was ten, Jan's recall of her feelings of disillusionment as a teacher of English, or Brian's recollection in the same chapter of his Father's pride in him as a learner, all illuminate social structures and behaviours through our individual perspectives. While the parallel review and discussion situates and connects those experiences within the wider context of the relevant structures such as family and the education system, the fact that we have chosen to tell these stories in the way we do is equally telling. The presentation and discussion of data in Chapter 5 begins as it were, in the future by considering the experiences of being a teacher educator through a number of themes or 'sites'. Subsequent sections move backwards in time through our perspectives on being teachers and being learners. While my own story presents a more chronologically conventional narrative it too follows this forwards and backwards perspective through my own narration (Appendix 2).

It was Dewey's (1903/1976) conception of analysis that develops into four analytical directions of inward, outward, forward and backward through the individual, the social/cultural, the future and the past, that helped me to consider Sartre's methodology in terms of this research. Pinar (1981) provides an example that offers links between Dewey's framework of analysis and Sartre's progressive/regressive method which he uses as a way of considering narrative autobiographical stories of the self 'harvested' through interview. Through this example (Pinar 1981) Dewey's four directions become 'regressive', 'progressive', 'analytic' and 'synthetic'. This maintains the continuity of analysis that Dewey saw as essential and links with notions of researcher 'signature and voice' as championed by Geertz (1973). A method of analysis that suits the narrative data and purpose of my study emerged from this 'bricolage' (Levi-Strauss, 1966).

de Creteau (1980) suggests that meaning emerging as narrative is one means of opposing institutional power. The 'intense singularities' of storytelling challenge the scientific discourse as it attempts to eliminate 'time's scandals:'

> Nonetheless they return over and over again, noiselessly and surreptitiously, and not least within the scientific activity itself: not merely in the form of the practices of everyday life which go on even without their own discourse, but also in the sly and gossipy practices of everyday storytelling…a practical know-how is at work in these stories, where all the features of the 'art of memory' itself can be detected…the art of daily life can be witnessed in the tales told about it (p.42).

Whether they are collected by others or we record them ourselves, if the researcher remains visibly central the tales are always autoethnographic, and that's where I'm calling from.

REFERENCES

Alexander, A. J., Craft, M., & Lynch, J. (1984). *Change in teacher education: Context and provision since Robbins.* Eastbourne: Holt, Rinehart and Winston.

Anderson, L. (2006). Analytic autoethnography. *Journal of Contemporary Ethnography,* 35, 373–395.

Anderson, N. (1923). *The Hobo: The sociology of the homeless man.* Chicago: Chicago University Press.

Antikainen, A., Houtsonen, J., Houtelin, H., & Kauppila. J. (1996). *Living in a learning society: Life-histories, identities and education.* London: Falmer.

Antoniou, M. (2002). *Writing my body: Exploring methods of articulating embodiment.* Unpublished PhD thesis, University of Manchester.

Atkinson, P. A., Coffey, A., & Delamont, S. (2003). *Key themes in qualitative research: Continuities and change.* Walnut Creek, CA: AltaMira Press.

Bailey, B., & Robson, J. (2002). Changing teachers: A critical review of recent policies affecting the professional training and qualifications of teachers in schools, colleges and universities in England. *Journal of Vocational Education and Training,* 54(3), 325–342.

Ball, J., & Goodson, I. F. (Eds.). (1985). *Teachers' lives and careers.* London: Falmer.

Ball, S. J. (2003). The teacher's soul and terrors of performability. *Journal of Education Policy,* 18, 215–228.

Basit, T. N. (1997). *Eastern values, Western milieu: Identities and aspirations of adolescent British Muslim girls.* Aldershot: Ashgate.

BBC. (1991). *Writers revealed,* BBC Radio 4, June 27, 1991.

Bochner, A. P. & Ellis, C. (1996). Taking ethnography into the 21st century (Special Issue). *Journal of Contemporary Ethnography,* 25(1), 3-5.

Bottery, M., & Wright, N. (2000). The directed profession: Teachers and the state in the third millennium. *Journal of In-Service Education,* 26(3), 475–487.

Brisard, E., Menter, I., & Smith, I. (2006). Discourses of partnership in initial teacher education in Scotland: Current configurations and tensions. *European Journal of Teacher Education,* 29, 49–66.

Britzman, D. P. (1991). *Practice makes practice: A critical study of learning to teach.* Albany, NY: State University of New York.

Brock, C. (1996). *Global perspectives on teacher education.* Wallingford: Triangle.
Brookfield, S. D. (1995). *Becoming a critically reflective teacher.* San Francisco: Jossey-Bass.
Bruner, J. (1986). *Actual minds, possible worlds.* Cambridge, MA: Harvard University Press.
Bruner, J. (1990). *Acts of meaning.* Cambridge, MA: Harvard University Press.
Bullough, R. V. (1989) *First year teacher: A case study.* New York: Teachers College Press.
Bullough, R. V., Knowles, J. G., & Crow, N. A. (1992). *Emerging as a new teacher.* New York: Routledge.
Burn, K. (2006). Promoting critical conversations: The distinctive contribution of higher education as a partner in the professional preparation of new teachers. *Journal of Education for Teaching,* 32(3), 243–259.
Carver, R. (1993). *Where I'm calling from.* London: Harvill.
Chryst, C., Lassonde, C., & Mckay, Z. (2008). The invisible researcher: New insights into the role of collaboration in self-study. In M. L. Heston, D. L. Tidwell, K. K. East, & L. M. Fitzgerald (Eds.), *The seventh international conference on self-study of teacher education practices. Pathways to change in teacher education: Dialogue, diversity and self-study* 50-54 Herstmonceux Castle, East Sussex, UK: S-Step/University of Northern Iowa.
Clandinin, D. J., & Connelly, F. M. (1986). Rhythms in teaching: The narrative study of teachers' personal practical knowledge of classrooms. *Teaching and Teacher Education,* 2(4), 377–387.
Clandinin, D. J., & Connelly, F. M. (1987). Teacher's personal knowledge: What counts as personal in studies of the personal? *Journal of Curriculum Studies,* 19(6), 487–500.
Clandinin, D. J., & Connelly, F. M. (1991). Narrative and story in practice and research. In D. A. Schon (Ed.), *The reflective turn: Case studies in and on educational practice* 258-281. NY: Teachers College Press.
Clandinin, D. J., & Connelly, F. M. (1994). Personal experience methods. In N. K. Denzin, & Y. S. Lincoln (Eds.), *Handbook of qualitative research.* 413-427. Thousand Oaks, CA: Sage.
Clandinin, D. J., & Connelly, F. M. (1995). Narrative and education. *Teachers and Teaching: Theory and Practice,* 1(1), 73–85.
Clandinin, D. J., & Connelly, F. M. (1999). Narrative inquiry. In J. P. Keeves, & G. Lakomski (Eds.), *Issues in educational research* 132-140 Kidlington, Oxford: Pergamon.
Cohen, R. M. (1991). *A lifetime in teaching: Portraits of five veteran high school teachers.* New York: Teachers College Press.
Connelly, F. M., & Clandinin, D. J. (1988). *Teachers as curriculum planners.* Toronto, ON: OISE Press.
Connelly, F. M., & Clandinin, D. J. (1990). Stories of experience and narrative inquiry. *Educational Researcher,* 19(5). 2–14.
Connelly, F. M., & Clandinin, D. J. (2001). Exploring the landscape of Canadian teacher education. *Asia Pacific Journal of Teacher Education and Development,* 4(1), 1–11.
Connelly, F. M., Clandinin, D. J., & He-Ming-Fang (1997). Teacher's personal practical knowledge on the professional knowledge landscape. *Teaching and Teacher Education,* 13(7), 665–674.
Crafton, L., & Smolin, L. (2008). The language of collaboration: Moving beyond self and other. In M. L. Heston, D. L. Tidwell, K. K. East, & L. M. Fitzgerald (Eds.), *The seventh international conference on self-study of teacher education practices. Pathways to change in teacher education: Dialogue, diversity and self-study* 82-87 Herstmonceux Castle, East Sussex, UK: S-Step/University of Northern Iowa.
Davies, C. A. (1999). *Reflexive ethnography: A guide to researching selves and others.* London: Routledge.
Davis, F. (1959). The cabdriver and his fare: Facets of a fleeting relationship. *American Journal of Sociology,* 65(1), 58–65.
de Certeau, M. (1980). On the oppositional practice of everyday life. *Social Text,* 1(3), 3-43.
Deegan, M. J. (2001). The Chicago school of ethnography. In P. Atkinson, A. Coffey, S. Delamont, J.Lofland, & L. Lofland (Eds.), *Handbook of Ethnography* 11-25 Thousand Oaks, CA: Sage.
Dent, H. C. (1975). *The training of teachers in England and Wales.* London: Hodder and Stoughton.

CHAPTER 2

Denzin, N. K. (1989). *Interpretive biography*. Newbury Park: CA, Sage.
Denzin, N. K. (1997). *Interpretive ethnography: Ethnographic practices for the 21st Century*. Thousand Oaks, CA: Sage.
Denzin, N. K. (2001). *Interpretive interactionism*. London: Sage.
Denzin, N. K. (2006). Deja vu all over again. *Journal of Contemporary Ethnography*, 35, 419–429.
Denzin, N. K., & Lincoln, Y. S. (Eds.). (1994). *Handbook of qualitative research*. Thousand Oaks, CA: Sage.
Denzin, N. K., & Lincoln, Y. S. (Eds.). (2000). *Handbook of qualitative research*. Thousand Oaks, CA: Sage.
DES (1972a). *Education: A framework for expansion*, White Paper. London: Department of Education & Science.
DES (1972b). *Teacher education and training* (The James Report). London: Department of Education & Science.
Dewey, J. (1903/1976). *Studies in logical theory*. Chicago: University of Chicago, Decennial.
DfE. (2010). *The importance of teaching*, Education White Paper. London: HMSO.
DfEE. (1996). *Lifelong learning: A policy framework*. London: HMSO.
DfEE. (1998). *Teaching: High status, high standards*. London: Department for Education and Employment.
DfES. (2005). *Standards in initial teacher training*. London: Department for Education and Skills.
Edwards, A., Gilroy, P., & Hartley, D. (2002). *Rethinking teacher education*. London: Routledge Falmer.
Elbaz, F. (1990). Knowledge and discourse: The evolution of research on teacher thinking. In C. Day, M. Pope, & P. Denicolo (Eds.) *Insights into teachers thinking and practice* 15-42 London: Falmer.
Eliot, T. S. (1933). *The use of poetry and the use of criticism*. London: Faber and Faber.
Ellis, C. (1998). Exploring loss through autoethnographic inquiry: Autoethnographic stories, co-constructed narratives, and interactive interviews. In J. H. Harvey (Ed.), *Perspectives on loss: A sourcebook* 49-61 Philadelphia: Taylor and Francis.
Ellis, C., & Bochner, A. P. (Eds.). (1996). *Composing ethnography: Alternative forms of qualitative writing*. Walnut Creek, CA: Alta-Mira.
Ellis, C., & Bochner, A. P. (2000). Autoethnography, personal narrative, reflexivity: Researcher as subject. In N. K. Denzin, & Y. S. Lincoln (Eds.), *Handbook of qualitative research* (2nd ed.) 773-769 Thousand Oaks, CA: Sage.
Ellis, C., & Bochner, A. P. (2006). Analyzing analytic autoethnography: An autopsy. *Journal of Contemporary Ethnography*, 35, 429–449.
Ellis, V. (2007). *Subject knowledge and teacher education*. London: Continuum International Pub Group.
Erben, M. (Ed.). (1998). *Biography and education: A reader*. London: Falmer.
Fentress, J., & Wickham, C. (1992). *Social memory*. Oxford: Blackwell.
Field, A. (1977). *V N: The life and art of Vladimir Nabakov*. New York: Crown.
Fiske, J. (1994). Audiencing: Cultural practice and cultural studies. In N. K. Denzin, & Y. S. Lincoln (Eds.), *The handbook of qualitative research* 189-198 Thousand Oaks, CA: Sage.
Fraser, R. (1984). *In search of a past: The manor house, Amnersfield, 1933–194*. London: Verso.
Furlong, J. (2000). *Higher education and the new professionalism for teachers: Realising the potential of partnership—A discussion paper*. London: CVCP, SCOP.
Furlong, J. (2005). New Labour and teacher education: The end of an era. *Oxford Review of Education*, 31(1), 119–134.
Furlong, J., & Smith, R. (Eds.). (1996). *The role of higher education in initial teacher training*. London: Kogan Page.
Flyvbjerg, B. (2001). *Making social science matter: Why social inquiry fails and how it can succeed again*. Cambridge: Cambridge University Press.
Garfinkel, H. (1967). *Studies in ethnomethodology*. Englewood Cliffs, NJ: Prentice Hall.

Geertz, C. (1973). *The Interpretation of cultures.* New York: Basic Books.
Gove, M. (2010). Gove to set out tougher teacher training rules, *The Daily Telegraph.* Nov 22, 2010.
Goffman, E. (1959). *The presentation of the self in everyday life.* New York: Doubleday, Anchor.
Goldman, A. (1993). Is that what she said? The politics of collaborative autobiography. *Cultural Critique*, Fall, 1993, 177–204.
Goodson, I. F. (1988). *The making of the curriculum.* London: Falmer.
Goodson, I. F. (Ed.). (1992). *Studying teachers lives.* London: Routledge.
Goodson, I. F. (2003). *Professional knowledge, professional lives: Studies in education and change.* Maidenhead: Open University Press.
Hamilton, M. L. (2008). Studying my practice: Exploring tensions in my teaching, my methodology and my theory. In M. L. Heston, D. L. Tidwell, K. K. East, & L. M. Fitzgerald (Eds.), *The seventh international conference on self-study of teacher education practices. Pathways to change in teacher education: Dialogue, diversity and self-study* 163-168 Herstmonceux Castle, East Sussex, UK: S-Step/University of Northern Iowa.Hargreaves, A. (1998). The emotional politics of teaching and teacher development. *International Journal of Leadership in Education*, 1(4), 315–336.
Hartley, D. (2000). Shoring up the pillars of modernity: Teacher education and the quest for certainty. *International Studies in Sociology of Education*, 10(2), 113–131.
Hayano, D. (1979). Auto-ethnography: Paradigms, problems, and prospects. *Human Organization*, 38, 113–120.
Hayler, M. (1989). *A publishing history of QueenSpark Books.* Unpublished BA (Hons.). Research Assignment, Brighton Polytechnic.
Heston, M. L., Tidwell, D. L., East, K. K., & Fitzgerald, L. M. (2008). Introduction, *The seventh international conference on self-study of teacher education practices. Pathways to change in teacher education: Dialogue, diversity and self-study* 173-177 Herstmonceux Castle, East Sussex, UK: S-Step/University of Northern Iowa.
Howey, K. R., & Zimpher, N. L. (1990). Professors and deans of education. In Houston, W. R. (Ed.). *Handbook of research on teacher education.* New York: Macmillan.
Huberman, M. (1993). *The lives of teachers.* London: Cassell.
Joyce, J. (1916). *A portrait of the artist as a young man.* New York: Ben Huebsch.
Kierkegaard, S. (1938). *The journals of Soren Kierkegaard.* Oxford: Oxford University Press.
Kitchen, J. (2008). The tenure trap as a tender trap: Balancing teaching and scholarship as an education professor. In M. L. Heston, D. L. Tidwell, K. K. East, & L. M. Fitzgerald (Eds.), *The seventh international conference on self-study of teacher education practices. Pathways to change in teacher education: Dialogue, diversity and self-study* 192-197 Herstmonceux Castle, East Sussex, UK: S-Step/University of Northern Iowa.
Korthagen, F., Loughran, J., & Lunenburg, M. (2005). Teaching teachers: Studies into the expertise of teacher educators. *Teaching and Teacher Education*, 21(2), 107–115.
Kundera, M. (2002). *Ignorance.* London: Faber.
Lanier, J., & Little, J. (1986). Research in teacher education. In M. C. Wittock (Ed.), *Handbook of research on teaching* 527-569 New York: Macmillan.
Levi-Strauss, C. (1966). *The savage mind.* Oxford: Oxford University Press.
Lincoln, Y. S., & Denzin, D. K. (2000). The seventh moment: Out of the past. In N. K. Denzin, & Y. S. Lincoln (Eds.), *Handbook of qualitative research* (2nd ed.) 1047-1065 London: Sage.
Lortie, D. (1975). *Schoolteacher: A sociological study.* Chicago: University of Chicago Press.
Loughran, J., & Russell, T. (Eds.). (1997). *Teaching about teaching: Purpose, passion and pedagogy in teacher education.* London: Falmer.
Lunenburg, M., Korthagen, F., & Swennen, A. (2007). The teacher educator as role model, *Teaching and Teacher Education*, 23, 586–601.
Lynch, J. (1979). *The reform of teacher education in the United Kingdom* (monograph). Guildford: The Society for Research into Higher Education, University of Surrey.

CHAPTER 2

Maguire, M. (2000). The state regulation of United Kingdom teacher education in the nineteenth century: The interplay of value and sense. *International Studies in Sociology of Education*, 10(3), 227–242.
McNair, A. (Chair). (1944). *Teachers and youth leaders* (The McNair Report). Board of Education. London: H.M.S.O.
Merrill, B. (1999). *Gender, identity and change.* Aldershot: Ashgate.
Miller, K. (1998). *Danger, doubt and distrust: An analysis of responses to new primary ITT curricula in primary science, BERA, Queens University.* Belfast: BERA, Education On-line.
Miller, K. (2007). *Women and science in primary teaching: A feminist post-structuralist analysis of power/gender conflicts.* Unpublished PhD thesis, University of Brighton.
Morrison, L., & Pitfield, M. (2006). Flexibility in initial teacher education: Implications for pedagogy and practice. *Journal of Education for Teaching*, 32(2), 185–196.
Murray, J. (2005). Re-addressing the priorities: New teacher educators and induction in higher education. *European Journal of Teacher Education*, 28(1), 67–85.
Murray, J., & Male, T. (2005). Becoming a teacher educator: Evidence from the field. *Teaching and Teacher Education*, 21(2), 125–142.
Nabakov, V. (1951). *Conclusive evidence.* New York: Harper & Brothers.
Nias, J. (1989). *Primary teachers talking: A study of teaching as work.* London: Routledge.
Noel, P. (2006). The secret life of teacher educators: Becoming a teacher educator in the learning and skills sector. *Journal of Vocational Education and Training*, 58(2), 151–170.
Osler, A. (1997). *The education and career of black teachers: Changing identities, changing lives.* Open University Press: Bristol.
Pinar, W. (1981). Whole, bright, deep with understanding: Issues in autobiographical method and qualitative research. *Journal of Curriculum Studies*, 13(3), 173–188.
Plowden. (1967). *Children and their primary schools* (The Plowden Report). London, UK: Central Advisory Council for Education.
Polkinghorne, D. (1988). *Narrative knowing and human science.* New York: State University of New York Press.
Porter, J. (1996). The James Report and what might have been in English teacher education. In Brock, C. (Ed.). *Global perspectives on teacher education.* Wallingford: Triangle.
Putnam, R. T., & Borko, H. (1997). Teacher learning: Implications of new views of cognition. In B. J. Biddle, T. L. Good, & I. F. Goodson (Eds.), *International handbook of teachers and teaching* 1223-1296Dordrecht, The Netherlands: Kluwer Academic Publishers.
Raine, C. (2008). Look back in wonder. *The Guardian*, January 5, London.
Rich, A. (1987/1981). Toward a more feminist criticism, *Blood, bread and poetry: Selected prose 1979–1985.* London: Virago.
Richards, C., Simco, N., & Twiselton, S. (Eds.). (1998). *Primary teacher education: High status? High standards?* London: Falmer.
Richardson, L. (1994). Writing: A method of inquiry. In N. K. Denzin, & Y. S. Lincoln (Eds.), *Handbook of qualitative research* 516-529 Thousand Oaks, CA: Sage.
Ricoeur, P. (1984). *Time and narrative (1).* Chicago: University of Chicago Press.
Ricoeur, P. (1985). *Time and narrative (2).* Chicago: University of Chicago Press.
Ricoeur, P. (1988). *Time and narrative (3).* Chicago: University of Chicago Press.
Robbins, L. (1963). *Higher education* (Robbins Report). London: Parliamentary Report.
Rose, S. (1992). *The making of memory: From molecules to mind.* London: Bantam.
Rosen, H. (1993). *Troublesome boy.* London: English and Media Centre.
Rosen, H. (1998). *Speaking from memory: A guide to autobiographical acts and practices.* London: Trentham Books.
Roth, J. A. (1963). *Timetables: Structuring the passage of time in hospital treatment and other careers.* Indianapolis: Boobs-Merrill.
Rousseau, J. J. (1781/1953). *The confessions.* Harmondsworth: Penguin.

Russell, T., & Loughran, J. (Eds.). (2007). *Enacting a pedagogy of teacher education*. London: Routledge.
Russell, T., & Munby, H. (Eds.). (1992). *Teachers and teaching: From classroom to reflection*. London: Falmer Press.
Sartre, J. -P. (1963). *The problem of method*. London, Methuen.
Sartre, J. -P. (1982). *Critique of dialectical reason Vol 1: Theory of practical ensembles*. London: Verso.
Sartre, J. -P. (1993). *The family idiot: Gustave Flaubert 1821/1857, Vol 5*. Chicago: University of Chicago Press.
Sikes, P. J., Measor, L., & Woods, P. (1985). *Teacher careers: Crises and continuities*. London: Falmer.
Smethem, L., & Adey, K. (2005). Some effects of statutory induction on the professional development of newly qualified teachers: a comparative study of pre- and post-induction experiences. *Journal of Education for Teaching*, 31(3), 187–201.
Smith, J. K., & Deemer, D. K. (2000). The problem of criteria in the age of relativism. In N. K. Denzin, & Y. S. Lincoln (Eds.), *Handbook of qualitative research* 877-897 London: Sage.
Steedman, C. (1986). *Landscape for a good woman*. London: Virago.
TDA. (2007). *Professional standards for qualified teacher status and requirements for initial teacher training*. London: Training and Development Agency.
Tedlock, B. (1991). From participant observation to the observation of participation. *Journal of Anthropological Research*, 41, 69–94.
Thompson, P. (1978). *The voice of the past: Oral history*. Oxford: Oxford University Press.
Thomson, A. (1994). *Anzac memories: Living with the legend*. Oxford: Oxford University Press.
Tillema, H., & Kremer-Hayon, L. (2005). Facing dilemmas: Teacher-educators ways of constructing a pedagogy of teacher education. *Teaching in Higher Education*, 10, 203–217.
Tillmann-Healy, L. (1999). *Life projects: A narrative ethnography of a gay-straight friendship*. Unpublished doctoral dissertation, University of South Florida.
Tyler, S. (1986). Post-modern ethnography: from document of the occult to occult document. In J. Clifford, & G. E. Marcus (Eds.). *Writing culture: The poetics and politics of ethnography* 122-140 Berkeley: University of California Press.
Van-Maanen, J. (1988). *Tales of the field*. Chicago: University of Chicago Press.
Weber, K. (1998). *Life history, gender and experience*. Frederiksberg: Roskilde University Press.
Weber, S., & Mitchell, C. (1995). *That's funny, you don't look like a teacher: Interrogating images and identity in popular culture*. London: Falmer.
Weinstein, D., & Weinstein, M. A. (1991). Georg Simmel: Sociological flaneur bricoleur. *Theory, Culture & Society*, 8, 151–168.
West, L. (1996). *Beyond Fragments: adults, motivation and higher education*. London: Taylor and Francis.
West, L., Alheit, P., Anderson, A, S., & Merrill, B. (2007). *Using biographical and life history approaches in the study of adult and life-long learning: European perspectives*. Frankfurt: Peter Lang.
Wideen, M. F., Mayer-Smith, J., & Moon, B. (1998). A critical analysis of the research on learning to teach: Making the case for an ecological perspective on inquiry. *Review of Educational research*, 68(2), 130–178.
Windschitl, M. (2002). Framing constructivism in practice as the negotiations of dilemmas. *Review of Educational Research*, 72, 131–177.
Winter, C. (2000). The state steers by remote control: standardising teacher education. *International Studies in Sociology of Education*, 10(2), 153–175.
Woolf, V. (1943). *The waves*. London: Hogarth Press.
Yeo, S. (1988). Difference, autobiography and history. *Literature and History*, 14(1), 37–35.

CHAPTER 3

CONDUCTING THE RESEARCH

In the spring of 1969, when I was 10, I became aware that my father was unwell. He spoke to us about the difficulty he was having eating his food. The doctor diagnosed an ulcer and then a hernia which needed an operation. He went to London for the operation and when he came back there was a more somber mood around the house. I must have gathered that he was very ill, although nobody told me this and I didn't really acknowledge it to myself. I didn't know he had cancer or what cancer was until after he died in June of that year at the age of 46. His death didn't bring our family close together in the way such events can. We seemed to go off into our own worlds to some extent. It didn't seem to have a dramatic effect on my education at the time. Or maybe it did but not in the way one would expect it to.

I went into a new class with my first male teacher for the final year of primary school. Although I must have failed the eleven plus at some point, that year was the happiest and most successful of any that I had at school. The teacher was a kind and creative young man who loved stories and poems and drama, especially musicals which he sometimes wrote himself. He worked hard at building up a class community which I felt part of. I remember that last year in primary school as a happy time when I did well at school and felt good about myself. I wrote stories, performed in plays and fell in love with history. It was the first time that I thought that being a teacher might be a pretty good job because Mr Marley was the first teacher I had met who seemed to really enjoy being a teacher. He seemed to like us and like his job. I liked him and started to like school. I began to be excited by learning things in a way I never had before. In retrospect, it was the lull before the storm that was not too far ahead but the 'epiphany' of that year, the discovery of the joy of learning and knowing and doing things for their own sake, the recognition of my need to learn and grow and express myself, served me well through the hard times to come, and eventually brought me back to the classroom as a teacher and a teacher educator when I met up again with Mr Marley and was able to tell him how I remembered that year in his class. While I failed the eleven plus I gained something much more useful than a place at a grammar school from this time.

I had wanted to go to the technical school because my brother was there but when I found out I was destined for the Secondary Modern school I didn't really mind. Mum seemed quite happy about it and I had some friends who were going there too. We went up the hill to have a look at the school during the summer holidays. It all seemed very modern surrounded by playing fields.

CHAPTER 3

METHODOLOGY INTO STRATEGY

This chapter tells the story of how the research was conducted by describing each phase of the process in detail and explaining why and how I decided to use these particular strategies and not others. Following an overview, each method of data collection is described and discussed in the chapter sections with reference to related literature and examples of each strategy. While the previous chapter includes a framework rationale and reasons for taking this overall approach, I will now illustrate each part of the process within the context of this particular project. My intention here is to show how the particular strategies I used engage the theories and philosophies of methodology discussed in the previous chapter and to give the reader a clear view of how research can be planned and conducted in terms of data production, collection and analysis. I explain how I considered and addressed ethical issues and how my thinking and strategies developed during the process.

OVERVIEW OF THE RESEARCH PROCESS

I started by writing a self-narrative of my own memories of being a learner which is discussed below. This piece of writing was then shared initially with two and eventually with six university-based teacher educators for them to read as a way of examining their own memories after reading mine, before I met each of them for a recorded interview discussion. These participants, who are properly introduced in Chapter 4, are colleagues, friends and associates who expressed an interest in being involved in the study. Following each interview I began transcription of the recording with some simultaneous note-taking and early analysis which initially considered 'turning point moments,' commonalities, and differences. A number of themes began to emerge which are discussed in Chapter 5. Two of the participants sent me further written contributions soon after our original discussions. I sent all six of them the transcription and recording of our discussion with an invitation for further written contributions. Some changes were then made to some transcripts before final versions were agreed by each participant. I received another three written contributions making five in all with one participant choosing not to add any more.

I had planned it pretty much like this, although in the early stages I thought we might meet as a whole group as I thought some direct interaction and sharing between the participants would be interesting and productive. I soon realised that group meetings of this kind need to be carefully organised and maintained and that the location of the various participants made this impracticable. I made adjustments and responded to circumstances within each part of the process as explained within the current chapter.

The relationship between my own experience and the experience of the other participants which was always difficult to identify and untangle, became one of the most interesting areas of the study. This was not an issue to be 'resolved'. How our narratives of self are informed by others' stories became the central theme and I found methodological support in the material on analytic autoethnography

CONDUCTING THE RESEARCH

(Anderson, 2006) with its insistence on including the voices of others in ethnographic work that begins with self-narrative.

To summarise my research 'bricolage' (Levi-Strauss 1966): I used a methodological approach discussed in Chapter 2 that is framed by Anderson's (2006) five features of:

- Complete member research
- Analytical reflexivity
- The narrative visibility of the researcher's self
- Dialogue with informants beyond the self
- A commitment to theoretical analysis

I developed my narrative analysis from Sartre's (1963) progressive/regressive method informed by Dewey (1976), Pinar (1981) and Denzin's (2001) critical interpretive approach also discussed in the previous chapter.

The methodological tools that I chose to use in each phase of the research are now explained and discussed within the narrative story of my study with examples and literature to support that process. This is necessarily detailed and concerned with both strategy and methodological theory as I need to tell the story of the decisions made, stepping out of the narrative along the way to gather some things together and muster support from writers living and dead, from near and far away in order to situate my thinking, my decisions and my strategies within the chosen framework.

WRITING

I had three interrelated intentions in beginning my research by writing the story of my own education:

- I wanted the process of writing itself to be a method of inquiry, exploration and discovery for me
- to make a qualitative account concerning how one teacher-educator remembered his own education which could be analysed to examine the autobiographical nature of his professional identity
- the story itself was to become part of the research process when shared with other-teacher educators with the intention of encouraging responses, although not particular responses, from the participants. This was also an effort to address the issues of reciprocity and equity in the research process as discussed below.

Writing My Own Story

I retrieved all my diaries, which I began in 1976, from out of the cupboard and made a list of family members, teachers and lecturers who I could interview about my education. I had in mind something like Ronald Fraser's *In Search of a Past* (1984) which had so changed the way I understood the past and the self. As explained in Chapter 2, Fraser makes the process of remembering a central theme

CHAPTER 3

by constructing his self-narrative from a number of perspectives. This fragmented and often contradictory narrative demonstrates the subjective and contextual nature of memory which becomes a way of understanding the present through the verisimilitude of the past. The voices within the text work like a collection of photographs spread out for the reader. While I wrote the my 'Telling Tale' without looking at my diaries other than to check a date or two, and I never did interview anyone from my past other than to ask my mum about a few specific questions which came up while I was writing, Fraser's structure did offer me a way of considering the data I gathered from the other participants whose narratives became witness to my profession rather than my life. Having read so many autobiographies and helped people to put theirs together I knew that stories about our pasts are always and can only be written by the people we are now.

Rosen says that stories live off stories:

> Of all the genres learned through language ... narrative is the genre we are most comfortable with. From a very early age we gather a rich experience of stories and learn more and more how they work, their methods and devices. So in our tellings, without our realising it, we use this hidden repertoire... We are all story tellers if only we are given the chance (Rosen, 1993, p151).

As soon as I started writing my tale I realised that what mattered here, was how I remembered and how I constructed my memories and how this narrative shapes my belief and practice within teacher education. Exploring how the story I make and remake about myself makes me who I am and how that influences my work as a teacher-educator began here. So I felt as though consulting the sources such as my diary or other people who were there was no more or less 'reliable' or 'valid' than any other method and that this sort of reliability was not the central issue here. Any attempt to make an 'accurate' history of my learning journey would be firstly in vain and secondly, to fundamentally miss the point. Bruner (1985, 1990) identifies autobiographical narrative as the central phenomena of what he terms as 'cultural psychology.' A particular view of the self is revealed through this window within a culture.

> What all these (reflexive autobiographical) works have in common is the aim and the virtue of locating self not in the fastness of immediate private consciousness but in the cultural-historical situation as well. (Bruner 1990, p.108).

I wrote my story over two weeks in September making changes and re-drafting as I went. I usually wrote long hand and added scribbles and crossing outs and then made further changes as I typed it into the computer. While I was unsure at this stage exactly when I would share my account with the other participants they were the readership I tried to keep first in mind while I was writing it. I struggled consciously with this as my primary audience competed in my thoughts with my supervisors, examiners and a future readership as well as with my past and present 'self' as it were, and all the other people, living and dead, who feature in the story.

I discussed the text with my supervisors soon after completion and made some minor changes for clarification before sending it to my first participant as part of the small pilot study discussed later in this chapter.

Writing as a Research Method and Method of Inquiry

In this section I discuss the process of writing itself as a method of inquiry drawing upon a range of literature to illuminate and situate my perspective and approach during the first phase of research.

While the story became my first piece of data and then part of my method through sharing it with others, writing it was firstly what Richardson (2000) terms as a 'Creative Analytic Practice' where process and product are displayed as deeply intertwined.

Scardamalia and Bereiter (1994) illuminate the particular ways in which our thoughts and knowledge are enhanced by writing and why it is different from thinking things over or talking to someone. Importantly, they argue and illustrate that none of the cognitive benefits often attributed to the process of writing happen automatically as a consequence of written composition. It is the dialectical process in writing, the tension between the content of what a writer wants to say and the required structure that leads to a deepening of reflective thought.

Donaldson (1978) followed and then added to Piaget's view (1953) in suggesting that the written form is a key factor in the development of higher reasoning abilities:

> ... those very features of the written word which encourage awareness of language may also encourage awareness of one's own thinking and be relevant to the development of intellectual self-control. (Donaldson 1978 p.5).

Bruner (1985) describes the radical change from 'maximally inner speech to maximally written speech' in becoming a writer. Vygotsky (1962) described it as 'a deliberate structuring of the web of meaning'. I remain convinced by Vygotsky's emphasis (Vygotsky 1962) on the role of language in enabling a learner to reflect on their own mental functioning, and Bruner's description of 'the mind turning back on itself' (Bruner, 1985) in how the development of abstract thought in the process of acquiring concepts, ideas and theories becomes conscious reflection on previous learning and experience. Language itself becomes the object as well as the means of reflection at such a point although given the inseparable nature of any individual's acquisition of literacy from the specific cultural capital of the society they live in this cannot be seen as a solely individual process. Of course, Vygotsky's descriptions incorporate and insist on the social as being an embedded part of individual development (Wertsch, 1985).

If writing becomes part of the process of developing reflective thinking Nicandor Parra's call to 'improve upon the blank page' takes on new meaning beyond poetry:

CHAPTER 3

> Write as you will
> In whatever style you like
> Too much blood has run under the bridge
> To go on believing one road is right
> In poetry everything is permitted
> With only this condition of course
> You have to improve upon the blank page. (Parra 1968 p.113)

It may yet be poetry alone that permits everything in writing but as discussed in the previous chapter the boundaries and traditions of writing in research and scholarship have also been expanded and redefined in recent years. Richardson (2000) further develops Vygotsky's view of the role of language in forming as well as expressing thoughts as she champions writing as a method of inquiry and research; a formative activity where we write to find something out and to learn something that we didn't know before. She acknowledges the power of dominant academic writing styles based on the static social world imagined by earlier generations of scholars.

Richardson (2000) argues convincingly for writing as a 'creative analytic practice' that invokes evocative analytical thinking entailed within the construction of text. With Denzin (Denzin and Lincoln, 2000, Denzin, 2006) and with Ellis and Bochner (2000, 2006), Richardson demonstrates that the analytical process takes place primarily within the planning and construction of a narrative. Therefore the crafting of the story is a process of analysis and the story itself represents that analysis at a particular point.

This raises some fundamental questions concerning epistemology and validity but if writing about the self is creative and analytic all on its own and no longer an alternative or experimental research method its validity comes not from notions of 'truth' and 'triangulation' but from 'verisimilitude' and interest. Richardson's (2000) central image of the crystal rather than the rigid, two-dimensional triangle as a frame of validity offers a wide avenue of possibilities in using writing as a way of knowing as it:

> ...combines symmetry and substance with an infinite variety of shapes, substances, transmutations, multidimensionalities, and angles of approach. Crystals grow, change, alter, but are not amorphous. Crystals are prisms that reflect externalities *and* refract within themselves, creating different colours, patterns, and arrays, casting off in different directions. What we see depends upon our angle of repose. Not triangulation, crystallisation
> (Richardson, 2000 p.934).

I highlight this perspective at this point rather than in the previous review chapter because it relates directly to the particular research strategy used in my research and illustrates my aims and my own perspective towards the inquiry.

CONDUCTING THE RESEARCH

In the Middle of the Story

'You will have to excuse what might at first seem like self-indulgent digression but I need to make this journey to gather up a few things that I want to say' (Potter 1994 p.41).

My 'Telling Tale' is a particular type of writing of course. I describe it as a self-narrative. It is a story, or a set of stories from my life; a narrative of my growth as a learner that contains much more than stories about school. It is a sort of autobiography with a theme that remains loosely within the stories. My narrator's voice moves forwards and backwards in time in a kind of analysis with the narrative as the story unfolds. Writing this felt strange at times, as though the character in the story was someone else. I seemed to know how to write this story. It was a story I thought I already knew but I came to know the story in a new way as I wrote it. As Goodson (1992, 2003) has argued, we gain understanding of ourselves through our understandings of context including the context of professional identity and policy frameworks.

How researchers might put themselves in their texts and with what consequences became a central theme of the research process. The challenge for me was to use writing to explore my past by making a narrative that might nurture my own individuality, still lay claim to knowing something and be shared with others as part of my research method. I did not see the fact that memories reveal more about our current circumstances than they do about our past as a problem or restriction as one of the key foci of my work is the current circumstances of teacher educators.

Bruner's (1990, p108) recognition that the Self must be 'treated as a construction that, so to speak, proceeds from the outside in as from the inside out, from culture to mind as well as from mind to culture', has deep resonance for me. The process of writing my 'telling tale' allowed me to consider the reflexive nature of the story and my own capacity and limitations in turning round on the past and altering the present in what Gergen (1973) described as the 'dazzling' human capacity to imagine alternatives.

Polkinghorne puts it like this:

> We achieve our personal identities and self-concept through the use of narrative configuration and make our existence into a whole by understanding it as a single unfolding and developing story. We are in the middle of our stories and cannot be sure where they will end.
>
> (Polkinghorne, 1988, p.150)

DEVELOPING THE FRAMEWORK

A set of principles emerged for me that seemed apposite not only to this part of my work but to the research as a whole:

- a life is created not recorded by self-narrative (Bruner and Weisser, 1991);
- autobiographical writing is a way of construing and then continually reconstruing experience, (Rosen, 1998, p90) and itself becomes part of experience;

CHAPTER 3

- understanding of the self is informed by our developing perceptions of the lived context including the professional and policy context: a relational dialogue which Goodson (1992, 2003) frames as 'genealogies of context;'
- only patches and glimpses of a more general and total, changing narrative about life can ever be revealed;
- conversions, awakenings, turning points, what Denzin (2001) calls 'epiphanies' emerge in the process of writing and sharing self-narrative and form key passages that stimulate responses in others.

I return to these principles in the final chapter of this book.

If writing about writing my own story of being a learner reveals a genealogy of my understanding of writing (Clark and Ivanic, 1997) – a meta story of how the method evolved, this must also be recognised as part of the same iterative and temporal process. Writing the story changed me; it allowed me to 'know' the story in a new way and to know something new without claiming to know everything as Richardson (1998) puts it.

While I wanted to begin with my own experiences I wanted to examine the themes that emerged for me with others. I wanted to see what emerged for others that had not occurred to me. I wanted to examine the wider context through our linked and different stories.

I wanted to invite my readers to examine their own memories after reading mine.

SHARING

The Self-narrative Text as a Research Tool

Marcus (1994) describes autobiographical discourses as 'collaborations waiting to happen' and while we are as Polkinghorne (1988) says 'in the middle of our stories' in more ways than one, each autobiography is also an invitation for the reader to examine their own memories after reading the memories of another, for while the process of writing a self-narrative invokes memory and brings new understanding within a current context for the writer, it also opens this possibility for the reader.

The collaboration that is 'waiting to happen' links closely with Anderson's (2006) principal point of connecting self-narrative with the narrative of others in ethnographic study and emphasises the potential of the relationship between self-narrative and life history interview methods where the self-narrative of the researcher is foregrounded. Such collaborations can bring, as Carver suggests 'news from one world to another' (Carver et al., 1990 p52) and they can also encourage, expand and develop perspectives and understandings within particular cultures and groups such as that of teacher educators.

Having written my story the next step for me was to share it with other teacher educators and gather their responses to it as a way of examining the phenomena of teacher education and the way memories of our own and others' education, influence belief and practice in my chosen profession. This went against the grain of traditional qualitative research to a certain degree raising concerns about how my story might influence the other participants. I felt that as long as this was a clear and transparent process it would have real advantages over the pretence of a distanced and 'uncontaminated' research style and was consistent with Anderson's (2006) principles of the researcher being visible and active within the text and the process, being a complete group member and engaging in dialogue with others.

I was interested in how the participants might respond to my story as a way of exploring how the stories we hear and the stories we tell influence our beliefs and our work in ITE.

The Pilot

One of my participants, Jan, agreed to read my story as a way of testing the process. I sent her the story and then interviewed her the following week. I followed a schedule of prepared questions to begin with but the discussion seemed to take a more interesting course and Jan was keen to talk about how she remembered her childhood and her own teacher education and some particular experiences that she saw as influencing what she believed about education and how this had affected her work in teacher education. My story served a number of functions during our meeting: it provided a sort of 'backdrop', a beginning and an 'ice breaker'. Jan said later that she felt as though she knew me better for reading the story. It gave her a sense of trust. It was also clear what I was up to and she felt free to talk about her past on those terms. I felt that this was a successful interview approach that produced interesting data and examples of how professional understanding is formed and developed socially and collaboratively, while following some of the established principles of qualitative study such as openness and clarity (e.g. Cohen et al., 2000; Hammersley, 1993).

I met another participant, Sian, for an interview without having sent her the story. My intention at this stage was to compare responses with Jan to help me to decide when to share my story with the remaining participants. The interview with Sian began as much more of a question and answer discourse although it developed into a discussion where Sian asked me as many questions as I asked her. I gave Sian my story at the end of the interview and we spoke the following week. She said she would have preferred to read the story before interview as she would have been much clearer about where I was 'coming from.'

Considering Ethics

Both interviews provided rich data for me to consider and analyse. Feeling as though I had nothing to lose and much to gain I decided to send all the participants my story in advance of further interviews. This also seemed like a good ethical approach. Lather (1991 p5) writes of taking away some of the barriers that prevent people from speaking for themselves in aiming to stimulate 'a self-sustaining process of critical analysis and enlightened action'. I felt that by beginning with my own story and sharing it with the other participants I was laying some cards on the table by framing and explaining my study to an extent without seeking to

CHAPTER 3

dominate the discussion. Lather says that this approach requires 'open-mindedness, dialogue, explicitness and reciprocity' (ibid) echoing Oakley's famous call of 'No intimacy without reciprocity' (1981 p49) and Fay's (1977) assertion that research should be as much about encouraging self-reflection and deeper understanding on the part of the researched as generating knowledge. Lather's summary of the procedures to encourage reciprocity includes interactive interviews, self-disclosure, collaboration and dialogue between participants that negotiates meaning.

While, unlike the work of these writers, my approach did not put the social construction of gender at the centre of the inquiry, I was strongly influenced by poststructural- feminist perspectives (Munro, 1998). In foregrounding the self-narrative while developing a 'reflexive connection between the researcher's and participants' lives' (Ellis, 2004, p30), autoethnography challenges many traditionally gendered dichotomies such as heart/mind, emotional/rational, literary/analytical, personal/scholarly, descriptive/theoretical that poststructural-feminism seeks to erase (Burnier, 2006; Miller, 1991; Munro, 1998; Richardson, 1997). In sharing my own story I also challenged some of my own embedded feelings informed by traditional notions of masculinity which made me feel both vulnerable and empowered at times as I stepped out of the 'security' of the socially constructed framework of knowledge that I thought I knew.

TALKING AND HEARING

Munro (1998) develops Bakhtins's (1981) notion of the dialogic self and examines how her life history work with women teachers works at the intersection of autobiography, narrative and life history research. This seems to be where I too settled as the interview discussions proceeded. Ricoeur (1974) shows us that it is narrative that gives the events of the past a meaning they do not otherwise have. Narrative 'soothes us'. My interest was in the professional identity of teacher educators and how this is both formed and represented by narratives of experience. Identity and pedagogy, understood here as what these teacher educators know, believe and do is illuminated through the themes and interpretations of experience in Chapter 5. The point of my method in sharing my story prior to the interviews was aimed at exploring how one person's life history/story from life initiates or prompts and is prompted by another. My intention was to get close to both the people and the phenomena of teacher education so as to examine some of the experiences and the practices that make up the basic concerns. The point here is to enter into dialogue with individuals and encourage the reader to occupy the space of what Foucault calls the 'contextually grounded norm' (cited in Flyvbjerg, 2001 p63) of becoming and being a teacher educator.

Interviews

The individual interviews themselves are discussed in more detail in Chapter 4 with analysis and discussion of the data they produced in Chapter 5. The present section discusses how and why I adopted the strategies used.

CONDUCTING THE RESEARCH

I felt that the data from the two interview/discussions that had already taken place with Jan and with Sian should be included in the analysis. The central sequential difference between Sian's and the others was that she had not read my story before we met. She sent me some written material not long after our meeting when she had read the story. I felt the material from our meeting and her writing was too rich to ignore and I did not think that the different sequence was the key factor here as long as I made this difference clear and kept it in mind when considering Sian's contributions.

While I kept the same sequence of: sharing my story – interview/discussion-written contribution, that I had established with Jan, with the remaining four participants, there were of course significant differences between all the interview/discussions. I met all of them at their places of work. While my story provided a beginning structure for the interviews the participants took differing attitudes to this with some referring back to it throughout while others used it more as a stimulus to talk more freely about their own experiences. I wasn't trying to create a scientifically 'fair test' where I asked each participant the same question at the same point in the interview. Each discussion involved just me and the participant, lasted between 52 and 68 minutes and was recorded on the same Phillips 9220 Digital recorder. Following the interviews I downloaded each recording onto my home computer for transcription which I did myself. I sent each participant a copy of the recording and the transcription having given them full rights of veto over anything concerning themselves that they did not want to be included.

I met with Brian in early January and asked him for a written response at the end of the interview which he posted to me at the end of February. This set the pattern for the rest of the interviews with Peter, Jackie and Kay. Jackie did not make a further written contribution although she said that she would if 'you really need it.'

Interview Approach

I settled on a largely unstructured approach as I wanted the interviews to be free-ranging to a certain extent. The story and the explanation sheet framed things to a large extent so I did not use a written interview schedule after I met with Sian. I have done lots of interviews since I began local life-history work in the 1980s and been most influenced by the life-story and popular memory interview approaches (Popular Memory Group, 1982). I drew on elements from a combination of these for the interviews in this research by encouraging four key interactions during my discussions with the participants: between interviewer and interviewee which was initially facilitated by sharing my story and by our shared professional experiences in ITE; between individual experience and public policy such as legislation affecting practices in ITE; between the present and the past through discussion of our own experiences as learners and as teachers; and between memory and identity (Thomson, 1994).

Reading my story seemed to encourage trust and enthusiasm from all six of the participants even from those I had met only briefly prior to the interviews. They all welcomed my interest in their memories and experiences in different ways and enjoyed participating in the project as demonstrated by their willingness to make

CHAPTER 3

written contributions following the interviews. I tried to keep the interviews and the interview relationship open and as equitable as possible by talking about my own interests and experiences.

My purpose in these discussions was to find out about them and what they thought. I also wanted to examine what they thought about what they thought and how they felt, and how they saw this affecting their work. Key moments from my own story came up during each interview and I brought up three areas for discussion if they did not arise in the meetings: how they remembered their time in school including any teachers they thought had been especially influential on them; what they believed about teachers and teaching; and their role now as teacher educators. These were themes that had arisen for me as I wrote my own story and now seemed to offer a way of opening possibilities for the participants to reflect upon their own experiences as learners, as teachers and as teacher educators which provided me with a structure for the organisation of the data and discussion presented in Chapter 5.

Having completed the interviews and agreed the transcripts with all six participants I now had seven separate self-narratives including my own.

Participants' Writing

I received writing from five of the participants after the interview discussions. Jan's was unprompted. She said that reading my story and our discussion had got her thinking about her own learning history and how she thought it had influenced her as a teacher and a teacher educator. She wanted to pick up on one area that we had discussed and two that we had not talked about much directly.

Sian sent me her written piece after she had read my story following our discussion. She focussed on one issue which I had raised in my story and one issue that we had discussed and how it linked with her philosophy of life and teaching.

The quality of this material encouraged me to ask all the participants to email or send me something written after our discussions and from my meeting with Brian onwards I included this request during each meeting. Sometimes I suggested a theme or incident for the writing during our discussion, as with Kay who found it difficult to talk about a particular memory but said that she wanted to tell me about it. Sometimes I simply suggested that they send me something if they had any further thoughts. They all did except for Jackie. Peter sent his after a second invitation which I sent with the transcript and recording of our discussion.

The participants' written contributions vary in length between 854 and 1243 words. I didn't suggest any particular length. They all carry a similar open and honest character and style and I am struck by how intimate and trusting they appear to be. The combination of reading my story and our individual meetings as well as being aware of the aims, ideas and conduct of the project seems to have allowed the participants to feel secure and trusting. Giving them final veto on any material concerning them allowed for an open contribution with the opportunity for retraction later. I also think that although we are based in a number of schools of education I was able to establish a collegiate relationship with the participants and that they wanted to contribute towards research within ITE and have their stories heard.

The written contributions allowed me to further develop my analysis and discussion around a number of themes which are explored in Chapter 5.

Reading and Representing

I now had 12 sets of data to analyse and represent: my own story, 6 interview transcripts and 5 pieces of writing from the participants. Working within Anderson's (2006) framework for analytic autoethnography I shared a commitment to an analytic agenda, although I agree with Denzin (1997, 2006) that narrow definitions of empiricist models of analysis risk reproducing inappropriate images of a positivist reader and an objective truth that needs to be revealed through research.

I chose to use a narrative analysis developed from Sartre's (1963) progressive/regressive method and Denzin's (2001) critical interpretive approach that required me to look forward from particular memories and accounts in the data towards a perceived conclusion or consequence of those experiences, decisions and actions, and then to look back towards the historical, cultural and biographical conditions that moved the narrator. The intention is to situate the memory and interpretation of actions in time and space, illuminating the uniqueness of the individual while revealing commonalities of the sub-culture (Sartre 1963 pp85–166).

I read through the interview material seeking commonalities and differences and identified three key areas from the data: being a learner, being a teacher and being a teacher educator. Using the progressive/regressive method of analysis I then wrote the presentation of data with a narrative analysis that forms the three sections of Chapter 5. In representing the data in this way I am employing more of a narrative analysis than an analysis of narrative (Polkinghorne, 1995) but I draw to a certain extent on both of these models. The emplotted self-narrative (Ricoeur, 1988) of my tale is the outcome of the narrative analysis of my own story. To reach a 'best fit' presentation represented through the pattern of the themed sections of Chapter 5 however, I followed a more paradigmatic search for themes and concepts which were deductively derived from the interview data. While I did not produce a unifying narrative to represent them, the participants' stories can be followed through the themed sections revealing a number of narratives which intersect at various points which I discuss as they emerge.

This offers a picture of ITE 'culture in practice' (Fiske, 1994 p195) by placing sets of experiences and perspectives alongside each other. The model works upward and outward from the individual self-narratives gathered through the writing and through interviews, towards the larger set of meanings that operate in the particular context of teacher education within university schools of education.

CHAPTER 3

SUMMARY

In this chapter I have told the story of how the 12 sets of data which inform Chapter 5 were produced, collected and analysed by describing each phase of the process in detail and explaining why and how I decided to use these particular strategies and not others.

The methods I used have been described and discussed with reference to related literature and examples of each strategy to show how the particular approaches I used engage the theories and philosophies of methodology discussed in Chapter 2 and to give the reader a clear view of how the research was planned and conducted.

REFERENCES

Anderson, L. (2006). Analytic autoethnography. *Journal of Contemporary Ethnography*, 35, 373–395.
Bakhtin, M. (1981). *The dialogic imagination*. Austin, TX: University of Texas Press.
Bruner, J. (1985). Vygotsky: A cultural and historical perspective. In Wertsch, J. (Ed.). *Culture, communication and cognition: Vygotskian perspectives* 21-35 Cambridge: Cambridge University Press.
Bruner, J. (1990). *Acts of meaning*. Cambridge, MA: Harvard University Press.
Bruner, J., & Weisser, S. (1991). The invention of self: Autobiography and its forms. In D. R. Olson, & N. Torrence (Eds.), *Literacy and orality*. 129-148 Cambridge: Cambridge University Press.
Burnier, D. (2006). Encounters with the self in social science research: A political scientist looks at autoethnography. *Journal of Contemporary Ethnography*, 35, 410–418.
Carver, R., Gentry, M. B., & Stull, W. L. (1990). *Conversations with Raymond Carver*. University of Jackson, MS: University Press of Mississippi.
Clark, R., & Ivanič, R. (1997). *The politics of writing*. London: Routledge.
Cohen, L., Manion, L., & Morrison, K. (2000). *Research methods in education*. London: Routledge/Falmer.
Denzin, N. K. (1997). *Interpretive ethnography: Ethnographic practices for the 21st century*. Thousand Oaks: CA, Sage.
Denzin, N. K. (2001). *Interpretive interactionism*. London: Sage.
Denzin, N. K. (2006). Deja vu all over again. *Journal of Contemporary Ethnography*, 35, 419–429.
Denzin, N. K., & Lincoln, Y. S. (Eds.). (2000). *Handbook of qualitative research*. Thousand Oaks, CA: Sage.
Dewey, J. (1903/1976). *Studies in logical theory*. Chicago: University of Chicago, Decennial.
Donaldson, M. (1978). *Children's mind*. London: Fontana Press.
Ellis, C. (2004). *The ethnographic I: A methodological novel about autoethnography*. Walnut Creek, CA: AltaMira Press.
Ellis, C., & Bochner, A. P. (2000). Autoethnography, personal narrative, reflexivity: Researcher as subject. In N. K. Denzin, & Y. S. Lincoln (Eds.), *Handbook of qualitative research* (2nd ed.) 773-769 Thousand Oaks, CA: Sage.
Ellis, C., & Bochner, A. P. (2006). Analyzing analytic autoethnography: An autopsy. *Journal of Contemporary Ethnography*, 35, 429–449.
Fay, B. (1977). How people change themselves: The relationship between critical theory and its audience. In Ball, T. (Ed.). *Political theory and praxis* 200-233 Minneapolis, MN: University of Minnesota.
Fiske, J. (1994). Audiencing: Cultural practice and cultural studies. In N. K. Denzin, & Y. S. Lincoln (Eds.). *The handbook of qualitative research* 189-198 Thousand Oaks, CA: Sage.
Flyvbjerg, B. (2001). *Making social science matter: Why social inquiry fails and how it can succeed again*. Cambridge: Cambridge University Press.

Fraser, R. (1984). *In search of a past: The manor house, Amnersfield, 1933–194*. London: Verso.
Gergen, K. J. (1973). Social psychology as history. *Journal of Personality and Social Psychology*, 26, 309–320.
Goodson, I. F. (Ed.). (1992). *Studying teachers lives*. London: Routledge.
Goodson, I. F. (2003). *Professional knowledge, professional lives: Studies in education and change*. Maidenhead: Open University Press.
Hammersley, M. (Ed.). (1993). *Educational research: Current issues* (Vol. 1). London: Paul Chapman in association with the Open University.
Lather, P. (1991). *Getting smart: Feminist research and pedagogy with/in the postmodern*. London: Routledge.
Levi-Strauss, C. (1966). *The savage mind*. Oxford: Oxford University Press.
Marcus, L. (1994). *Autobiographical discourse*. Manchester: Manchester University Press.
Miller, N. K. (1991). *Getting personal: Feminist occasions and autobiographical acts*. New York: Routledge.
Munro, P. (1998). *Subject to fiction: Women teachers' life history narratives and the cultural politics of resistance*. Buckingham: Open University Press.
Oakley, A. (1981). Interviewing women: A contradiction in terms. In H. Roberts (Ed.), *Doing feminist research* 30-61 London: Routledge and Kegan Paul.
Parra, N. (1968). *Poems and anti-poems*. London: Jonathan Cape.
Piaget, J. (1953). *Logic and psychology*. Manchester: Manchester University Press.
Pinar, W. (1981). Whole, bright, deep with understanding: Issues in autobiographical method and qualitative research. *Journal of Curriculum Studies*, 13(3), 173–188.
Polkinghorne, D. (1988). *Narrative knowing and human science*. New York: State University of New York Press.
Polkinghorne, D. (1995). Narrative configuration in qualitative analysis. In Hatch, A., & Wisniewski, R. (Eds.). *Life history and narrative* 5-23 London: Falmer.
Popular Memory Group. (1982). Popular memory: Theory, politics, method. In R. Johnson, & G. McLennan (Eds.), *Making histories: Studies in history, writing and politics* 75-86 London: Hutchinson.
Potter, D. (1994). *Seeing the blossom*. London: Faber and Faber.
Richardson, L. (1997). *Fields of play: Constructing an academic life*. New Brunswick, NJ: Rutgers University Press.
Richardson, L. (1998). Writing: A method of inquiry. In N. K. Denzin, & Y. S. Lincoln (Eds.), *Collecting and interpreting qualitative materials* 499-541 London: Sage.
Richardson, L. (2000). Writing: A method of inquiry. In N. K. Denzin, & Y. S. Lincoln (Eds.), *Handbook of qualitative research* 923-948 London: Sage.
Ricoeur, P. (1974). *The conflict of interpretations*. Evanston, IL: Northwestern University Press.
Ricoeur, P. (1988). *Time and narrative (3)*. Chicago: University of Chicago Press.
Rosen, H. (1993). *Troublesome boy*. London: English and Media Centre.
Rosen, H. (1998). *Speaking from memory: A guide to autobiographical acts and practices*. London: Trentham Books.
Sartre, J. -P. (1963). *The problem of method*. London: Methuen.
Scardamalia, B. M., & Bereiter, C. (1994). Development of dialectical processes in composition. In B. Stierer, & J. Maybin (Eds.), *Language, literacy and learning in educational practice*. Clevedon: Multilingual Matters in association with the Open University.
Thomson, A. (1994). *Anzac memories: Living with the legend*. Oxford: Oxford University Press.
Vygotsky, L. S. (1962). *Thought and language*. Cambridge, MA: The M.I.T. Press.
Wertsch, J. (1985). *Culture, communication and cognition: Vygotskian perspectives*. Cambridge: Cambridge University Press.

CHAPTER 4

NEIGBOURING VOICES

SECONDARY MODERN

Because the buildings were modern in design and the playing fields were extensive, I was quite happy to become one of the 500 pupils at the secondary modern school. I didn't have a feeling of failure or disadvantage about going there. I don't remember being aware that the boys and girls who went to the grammar schools were seen as superior or that they would be given greater opportunities and expected to take a higher path in life than we were. I was impressed by the facilities which were advanced compared to the primary school. I was in Form 1B within the 'A' to 'D' streaming system. I have never managed to find out exactly how the staff decided who went where when they first arrived at the school but I think it must have been based on primary school reports and eleven plus exam marks.

To begin with I did quite well with my school work and got involved in organised sport for the first time. I became the town schools boxing champion for my age and weight division and then broke my arm when I fell in the street. There were also more opportunities for bad behaviour and as the year progressed I started to get into trouble on a regular basis. I recall that winter of 1970/1971 as the time when things caught up with me. I think I started to reflect on things to a certain degree and it hurt. It made me angry but I didn't know who with. I got in with what my mum called 'a rough crowd' and I became one of the roughest. I was cautioned by the police and then put on probation after an appearance in juvenile court for breaking into a car.

Although I was 'suspended' from school early in my second year I remained interested in learning and enjoyed writing stories. I was aware that I had turned most of the teachers I knew against me and that they didn't like me much. My second year form tutor did seem to like me. He was an inspirational and committed English teacher who encouraged creative writing and class debates. He seemed to like us and care about what we had to say. I wrote stories that were about getting into trouble and dilemmas of loyalty. Mr Sacks who was in his mid-fifties did not tolerate or condone any disruptive behaviour in class or elsewhere but there was something of the non-conformist outsider about him. He encouraged us to question everything and channel our energies into positive activities. He was very open about being an atheist and a communist. When I wrote an essay on the subject of violence he made sure the head teacher knew about it and I received praise for my work in English and History.

Two important things happened and I had to make a decision. Firstly my friend Terry was sent to a local authority children's home when we were caught stealing a car together. I used to go to visit him there and I knew that I would soon be joining him if things continued in the way they were. I also knew that I didn't want to live there. Secondly I read a book by Emmett Grogan called Ringolevio: a life played for keeps (Grogan, 1972) . I bought it because the cover looked exciting and said it was 'The most amazing true-life adventure since Papillon.' Lots of books have influenced me since then but none more so than this dubious autobiography written like a novel in the third person. The key message for me at the age of 13 was that you could be tough and sensitive at the same time. Grogan had been a criminal who became a radical community activist in San Francisco in the 1960s. He took authority on and subverted the system. He was a counter-culture poet and street performer who linked art and action on his own terms. He had formed the Diggers group with others in Haight-Ashbury and organised free food for several years in Golden Gate Park: see (Coyote, 1999, Wolfe, 1971). On the back of the book Kenneth Allsop described Grogan as 'an alienated character ranging suspiciously from underworld to underground'[i] . He seemed to me like somebody who knew how to look after himself and help others. I needed to look after myself without feeling that I was losing face or being turned into someone that I didn't want to be. The loss of freedom that Terry was experiencing filled me with dread and stood in sharp contrast to what I saw at the time as the freewheeling, boundary-breaking outlaw life that Grogan described in such a dramatic and idiosyncratic way. I wanted to succeed without conforming and I wanted to be 'different'.

Grogan is the man who coined the phrase 'Today is the first day of the rest of your life'. I recognised that I needed to show some real independence and think about others as well as myself and I stopped getting into trouble with the police. I discovered other counter-culture writers and poets such as Kerouac, Ginsburg and Corso and started writing my own poems. For a while it looked as though I was going to do quite well at the school which became a comprehensive in 1973. I seemed to be finding a way to learn and study and stay out of trouble without feeling controlled by others. The school stopped boxing but started rugby and I was captain of the school team. Terry came home and I fell in love with a girl in my new form. She was keen on me too – for a while.

My interests in history and literature were combined through reading the work and biographies of writers and poets. I fashioned a sort of adolescent personal philosophy from a heady mix of communism, urban-anarchy and muscular romanticism which now that I consider it, was not as unusual then as it sounds now. There were certainly people a good deal older than I was cultivating something similar at the time. It only needed my girlfriend to tell me that she didn't want to see me anymore for life to become stranger than ever. I felt the full force of rejection and despair and fell into a self-destructive depression early in my final year of school. It was a case of things catching up with me again and the timing was bad. I started getting into trouble at school again and fell out with the new head teacher who suspended and then expelled me permanently in February 1975. I was supposed to go to another school but there was no way that was going to happen. I went to the careers office in town and mumbled about wanting to be a journalist but they told me I needed 'O' levels for that. I got a cash-in-hand job until July and then signed on the dole for the summer before starting work at a large bakery and bread factory in September. I did get the 'O' levels but not for another ten years.

INTRODUCING THE PARTICIPANTS

In this chapter I introduce the people who participated in the project with me. My intention is to now explain how they came to be involved and to present them here as the interesting and complex individuals they are, allowing the reader to establish a sense of them as unique characters who can be identified throughout the narrative analysis of Chapter 5. I want to avoid what Miller and Glassner (1997 p99–111) highlight as the dangers of representing individuals as 'subjects' who become 'mere data' leading to an apparent dismemberment of their individual identities which emerge only as theoretical patterns.

I composed these biographical sketches of each participant based upon our discussions and their writing and then agreed a final draft with each of them after they had made some alterations and additions. Each sketch begins with a quotation from either the interview with or the writing by the participant that we feel represents how they see themselves as teacher educators. A similar structure touching upon the participant's background, interests and career history frames each of these introductions along with a summary of their views on being a learner, being a teacher and being a teacher educator.

By listening to my professional neighbours and reading their stories I began to identify and know my own story more deeply. More importantly perhaps, I made connections with these teacher educators and our stories intertwined in many unexpected ways without losing their individuality. This allowed me to create the narrative analysis which forms Chapter 5, to create a new context for how I understood teacher education and to discover a sense of professional community that I had not felt before.

The table below summarises general background information about the participants

Name (chosen by participant)	Contribution to this research	Started teaching	Began work in ITE	Currently working (2009)
Brian	Interview (i): January 2008 Written story (s): February 2008	Secondary maths 1966 with Certificate in education	1992	University School of Education: Maths Education (part-time)
Jackie	i: January 2008 Did not write story	Primary 1982 (-85) with P.G.C.E	1988	University School of Education: University/School partnerships – liaison, research and writing

Table (Continued)

Jan	i: December 2007 s: January 2008	Primary 1980 with BEd	1998	University School of Education: English education and Education Studies
Kay	i: February 2008 s: February 2008	Primary/secondary special school for the deaf from 1957 without QTS (QTS through ATP from 1982)	1996	University School of Education: Special Needs Education (part-time)
Mike (researcher)	s: September 2008	Primary 1991 with P.G.C.E	2004	University School of Education: Education Studies
Peter	i: January 2008 s: February 2008	Post-compulsory education 1995	2004	University School of Education: ICT education
Sian	i: December 2007 s: January 2008	Secondary science 1976 (later RE specialist)	1991	University School of Education: Professional Studies, Education Studies, research and writing

SELECTING THE PARTICIPANTS

I had been talking with people about my developing interest in the pedagogy of teacher educators and how this is both formed and represented by narratives of experience for some time and a number of colleagues, friends and associates have expressed an interest in being involved. As the project became more focused for me, some criteria for participant involvement in the research began to emerge. Firstly I wanted to share experiences with university-based teacher educators who were currently directly involved with the education of students who are preparing to become teachers. This narrowed the potential participants down to nine people who I had talked with. Secondly I felt it was important that they were able to and genuinely interested in being involved as a way of examining this in this way for themselves and that they felt they would get something out of the experience as well as supporting my study. I did not seek a narrow rationale or close criteria for involvement beyond their professional position and practicable enthusiasm since I was aiming to illuminate and examine the experiences and memories of university based teacher educators, not for example a specialist area of teacher education, a particular institution or lecturers of a certain age.

After a number of correspondences and conversations, five participants who work in four different university schools of education agreed to be involved. One of these is a friend of a relative of mine who I have met several times over the years. I have worked in ITE with two of the others and met the other two at a conference in 2005. Another participant joined the project by contacting me when she heard about it from one of the others who she works with. While not a central requirement of my study, I was pleased that we work in several different universities since this study is not an investigation into a particular institution.

INTRODUCTIONS

The following introductions to each person appear in the order in which I interviewed them.

Jan: It's Higher Education Mike but Not as We Know It

Jan grew up in the South of England. She began a BEd (Hons) degree in London when she was eighteen. Following graduation she was a primary school teacher for eighteen years, working in four different schools during that time. Jan's particular passions in education are children's literacy and literature which she sees as the key skills and resources in learning and in life. Reading and stories have always been important to her and she describes herself as 'a whole book person' and believes that 'language is about communication and literacy, and language in English is about pleasure and enjoyment.'

Jan became a lecturer in a university school of education after she and her family moved to a new area when her partner began a new job in the late 1990s. She says that she had become disheartened by developments in primary education; especially the National Literacy Strategy which she felt encouraged a functional and narrow approach to the subject she most loves to teach. When the opportunity arose she made the change and applied for a job in teacher education. She moved to her current post in another university in 2001 attracted by what she saw as the innovative attitude towards English which remains her specialism within the teacher education work she does with undergraduate and post-graduate students. Her MA studies focused on the way in which children develop social understanding through hearing and reading stories, an area that she continues to research although she finds this difficult with a full teaching and student support timetable. Jan says she enjoys her job most of the time and sees it as a continuation and extension of the work she did as a teacher in schools rather than as new career. She positions ITE as somewhere between school and higher education or as higher education 'but not as we know it'.

She recognises the influence of her parents and of a particular teacher she had when she was 14 upon her own beliefs about teaching and learning. Her parents' belief in education and the rewards of hard work were a central motivation in doing well at school and she thinks that her love of books and stories came from them. Even so, it was Miss Cox, the English teacher, who made Jan 'see things in

CHAPTER 4

a new way' and from that time, being a teacher was all she ever wanted to do. Jan's narratives are punctuated by her feelings about the influence of the national literacy strategy and the literacy hour on school teaching which she says 'killed it' for her. While she describes many of the key decisions she has made as 'more personal than professional' she thinks that one of her motivations for moving into teacher education was to be able to influence new teachers in resisting narrow and prescriptive approaches to teaching English in particular. She recognises her own practical knowledge of schools as a resource for students and also the changing role of teacher educators in partnership with schools. A theme that emerged from our discussion was her own identification of herself as an expert in English rather than in Education. She sees some of the changes in ITE in recent years as being similar to those made in schools during the 1980s and 1990s. She does not take an especially epiphanic view towards the events of her life believing more in trends, shifts and currents than in critical moments and turning points.

Sian: Who do I think I Am?

Sian describes her background as working class. She grew up in an industrial town in the North of England, went to university at eighteen and gained a first class degree in English. From there she went straight to teacher training college to take a Secondary Science PGCE. She began her teaching career at a comprehensive school in London teaching science and religious education. She taught in two schools over a period of 15 years, becoming head of RE, deputy head and head of upper school before joining the school of education at a university. She did her MA in Education while teaching full time, gained her Doctorate in 2003 and has published several articles and chapters in books on different aspects of inclusive education. She is now a reader in education at a large university teaching on Postgraduate ITE and CPD courses while continuing to research and write.

Sian decided that she would like to be a teacher educator while she was taking her PGCE. Although it was 15 years before she began this stage of her career and it might not have happened at all if she had been successful in her applications to be a head teacher, she still feels that she was meant to do it and enjoys the job which she feels has a high status and an important part to play in education. She sees it as a very different role from being a school teacher but thinks it is important that teacher educators should have been school teachers themselves as 'you are changed forever by teaching.' She speaks of her 'faith' in education and her belief in the way it can transform people's lives as it has transformed hers. Her undergraduate experience was particularly important for Sian. She was influenced especially by two lecturers while she was at university who she remembers as outstanding and central to the formation of her pedagogical and epistemological principles which are based partly on what she describes as a 'poetic perspective of the possibilities of life.' It was at university where she feels that she found herself, decided who she wanted be and where she remembers feeling good about herself for the first time. She says that she 'saved' her own life and used education as a means of escape from a life and location she did not want to be part of. Helping others to make similar changes in their lives has been a motivating force in Sian's career as a teacher, teacher educator and educational researcher and writer.

While the circumstances of her childhood have driven Sian away from her past in some ways, she also identifies them as a continuing evocative resource which she draws upon for personal and professional energy and grounding. She views her own story as one of growth and change and looks back at her past self as someone she used to be. She is sometimes surprised at how things have developed for her as she never imagined she would be an academic and a published author and wonders with humour about who she thinks she is from time to time. For Sian the key agent for such transformation is the influence that human beings have upon each other, either directly or through the things we create such as art, music and literature.

Brian: 'I Knew That Would be a Great Way to Spend the Day; Helping People Find Things Out.'

Brian has been a senior lecturer in Mathematics Education at a university for 17 years. Before that he taught maths in a secondary school for 25 years having gained his degree in maths as a mature student. He completed an Ed Cert course, which he describes as 'grim' before becoming a teacher. He later took a PGCE and then an MA from the Open University while teaching full-time.

In retrospect Brian has come to see his education as a means of escape from a life in the steel works and probable unemployment in his home town in Wales: 'My brother is a good example. He stayed there and ended up in all sorts of trouble ...' He recognised early on that success at school was a way in which he could please his parents. He has very positive memories of a science teacher who first gave him the idea of being a teacher himself and strong views about the responsibility that teachers carry in creating an environment where learning can take place remembering a particular teacher who influenced his view on the profession: 'I knew that would be a great way to spend the day; helping people find things out.'

He was also influenced by stories of teachers facing and overcoming adversity in order to help young people improve their prospects in life such as *To Sir with Love* by E.H. Braithwaite: 'The way he had to win the youngsters over, get their respect. I taught in a school like that in London. You couldn't do much until they were on your side.'

Brian was a high achiever in school and chose to study mathematics at university because he thought it would be more useful in finding a job than his first love which is music. He says that while he has no regrets he does not feel 'special' at maths. He is glad that music has remained a serious hobby and pursuit for him rather than his profession but he has moments of wondering what might have been. Changes in his personal circumstances and the situation at work led to him leaving the school where he taught for 25 years and he still feels that he was badly treated by the school management and the local authority. He started teaching part-time at the university and now works with student teachers most of the week.

CHAPTER 4

For Brian the key issue for students who are preparing to be teachers is subject knowledge. While he recognises the importance of the classroom and school environment, relationships and the skills of teaching he believes that these mean very little unless the teacher has a good understanding of the subject they are teaching.

Although he feels he needed to get away from the area, Brian is very proud of his roots in many ways and sees himself as a Welshman living in exile. He describes himself as a disillusioned socialist and sees education as one of the many areas where the Labour Party has let people down. He still believes that the class analysis of society has much to contribute but also that history proves that Marxism cannot work in practice. While he thinks that life history and narrative study provides useful perspectives of the past and insights into individual personal and professional development, he is uncertain and somewhat sceptical about how accurate such accounts can ever be. For Brian there is always the need to test information of any kind against the facts.

Peter: 'You Need the Passion First. It's What Gets You Through. Why Do It Otherwise'

Peter's parents were teachers. His Father was the Head of a large secondary school in the midlands and his mother became deputy head of a primary school in the same town. Peter says that he 'resisted' going into teaching for a while and that his parents did not particularly encourage him in this direction although both he and his sister began QTS courses in the 1980s feeling as though 'there was nothing else we could really do.' Peter had worked for a publisher and as a customs officer before that gaining little satisfaction but a good knowledge of ICT. He began his Secondary ICT BA (Ed) when he was 25 but failed his second school-based teaching placement and dropped out of the course feeling that school teaching was not for him. He found the atmosphere on the course and in the schools 'mean-spirited and all about controlling the kids.' His ICT skills helped him to find work in post-compulsory education which he found to be a completely different and far more rewarding experience. He moved from further to higher education in 2004 and now works in ICT education with students preparing to teach in the secondary and post-compulsory sectors.

Peter describes himself as 'an active Christian socialist' but does not believe that theologies or philosophies of any kind should be imposed upon the young. He is concerned that the system of education in England is being increasingly manipulated into a means of social control, an enterprise he sees as both damaging and doomed to failure. He believes that real education should allow individuals to make individual choices and that this will in turn allow them to identify their own interests as inextricably linked to the interests of others. His own experiences make him feel that overly-competitive and commercially orientated systems of education will narrow our understanding of what education and learning are for. He strongly believes that people learn and teach best together in collegiate and collaborative ways and that the key requirement of being a successful teacher is a passion for learning and the subjects they teach: 'It's what gets you through. Why do it otherwise?'

Peter speaks of his own 'passion' for a better world as the driving motivation that brought him to teaching after a while and led him to continue to seek and find ways in which he could be a teacher and teacher educator after some set backs in his life and career. In Peter's opinion teacher educators have an intellectual and moral responsibility to do all they can in maintaining the values of independence and freedom in education and supporting human rights throughout the world.

Self-study and reflection have been an important aspect of Peter's personal and professional development and he was especially keen to be part of this project because he feels that we come to know ourselves individually and collectively through understanding our own stories and the way we construct them. He thinks that good personal and professional health comes from being able to build and strengthen self-esteem, by deconstructing our own stories using cognitive tools and strategies.

Jackie: 'I'm Still Trying to Work It All Out Really.'

Jackie did well at the private girls' school she attended on the south coast of England and at university where she read psychology. She travelled and worked abroad for several years taking part in school-based projects in India and Africa, valuable experiences that later formed the basis of her MA in Education. On her return to England she completed a primary PGCE and taught in school for three years before leaving to take her MA full time. She began work as a visiting lecturer on a teacher education course that year which she increased while researching and writing her PhD on child development and learning. She became a full time faculty member on completing her Doctorate which was later published. She continues to research and publish as well as being a course leader and working with undergraduate and post-graduate students of education on their dissertations and theses.

Jackie's work in ITE focuses upon partnerships with schools and encouraging students to develop and use their research skills as a way of expanding their understanding of learning and teaching and the ways in which schools work. She enjoys her work with students who are preparing to be teachers but is glad that she works with a variety of students including practicing teachers and other educational practitioners. While she thinks it is important for teacher educators to spend some time in schools and to keep up to date with what is going on, she does not see herself as a school teacher at heart. Her brief time as a teacher was an important part of her development as an educationalist: 'I don't see myself as a teacher who's moved 'up' in anyway. I've become an academic in education. That's not better or worse, higher or lower than being a teacher. It's a different job altogether. Along the way I had a number of important experiences that have made me who I am and helped me find out what I want to do and being a teacher was one of them.'

Jackie believes that she has a different, equally important role to the school-based mentors she works with in supporting the education of students of teaching.

CHAPTER 4

She says that she is still working it out, but she thinks that her role is to 'break into the cycles of repetition' that students and teachers can fall into by encouraging both students and practicing teachers to reflect upon and analyse their own and others' practice in order to challenge some of the assumptions that become established in education. Central to this is the ability to question one's own thinking and consider where your own ideas and beliefs have come from. The first few years of a teacher's career are the most important as far as Jackie is concerned and her research with NQTs has confirmed her view that university schools of education should be making a larger input to this phase of teacher education and development so as to provide opportunities for NQTs to continue to study education beyond the classroom.

For Jackie, the need to bring change to teacher education and school teaching is underpinned by her commitment to challenging the gendered power relations in society. Education has a particular role in resisting and reshaping the patterns of behaviour and understanding that marginalise and minimise women in relation to men. Stereotypical images of women school teachers reinforce this dynamic and continue to undermine education itself. She sees narrative as a social action that takes lives seriously and offers agency in making change happen through deeper understanding of oneself and ones culture.

Kay: 'I was Born to Be a Teacher.'

Kay works part-time as a teacher educator at a university in the Home Counties where she lives. She began this work when she retired as a teacher in a school for the deaf where she worked for nearly 40 years. The focus of Kay's work as a teacher was always in special schools of one sort or another and began when she was 17, although she was not awarded Qualified Teacher Status until she was 42.

Kay's work with students centres on strategies to support children with learning difficulties and overcoming potential barriers to learning as well as classroom organisation, the school environment, and building good relationships with pupils. She believes that all learners deserve an equal opportunity to learn and that inclusive, genuinely integrated education is the best way to achieve this. Although her own career as a teacher was spent exclusively in special schools she now feels that all children with different and varying needs should be taught together. She thinks that deaf and hearing children in particular can benefit from learning together in the same setting.

Being a teacher is all Kay has ever wanted to do. She used to teach the younger children at Sunday school when she was nine. She has never wanted to be a head or deputy head because: 'I always thought it would mean teaching less. It takes you out of the classroom which is where I've always wanted to be.' Equally, further or higher qualifications have held little interest for Kay: 'I only did the Cert Ed because it looked as though I might lose my job at one point.' She believes that teaching is about character and that the best teachers have a natural skill and aptitude that can't be taught. Teaching is her 'mission in life' and she feels that she was born to do it. It is the contribution she makes to society and to the children, families and now students who she works with. While she has never been an evangelist, she has always been very open about being a Quaker and comfortable with sharing her beliefs with her students and colleagues.

Kay believes that our stories are 'meant to be' in some ways and that while we have free choice and make our own decisions, fate plays the largest part in our overall destiny and that this is all part of a plan that we cannot hope to understand. The strongest influences on her decisions were her Father who encouraged her to be a teacher and the Father of a friend who told her about the Quaker movement and invited her to a meeting when she was a teenager. Helping others, especially those who she sees as less fortunate than herself has always been a central motivation for Kay as a teacher and now as a teacher educator. She sees her role in teacher education as ensuring that those who have difficulty with learning are not forgotten and remain at the forefront for those who are preparing to teach. She sees her own narrative as memories of key moments when certain truths were revealed to her and she was able to follow the path that had been planned on her behalf.

REFERENCES

Coyote, P. (1999). *Sleeping where I fall: A chronicle*. Washington, DC: Counterpoint.
Grogan, E. (1972). *Ringolevio: A life played for keeps*. London: Heinemann.
Miller, J., & Glassner, B. (1997). The inside and the outside: Finding realities in interviews. In D. Silverman (Ed.), *Qualitative research: Theory, practice and method* 99-112 London: Sage.
Wolfe, T. (1971). *The electric kool-aid acid test*. London: Bantam.

NOTES

[i] From the Sunday Times review of the book in 1972.

CHAPTER 5

A STORY FULL OF STORIES

WORK

The bakery has gone now, replaced by new business units, but if you drive by you can still see the wall I used to sit on waiting for the bus after work at my first job. If you keep going for a few minutes the next building you come to is the university where I was later employed as a senior lecturer in education. The distance between my first and my current jobs seems so far and yet so close, as though the puzzle of who I am is in the undulating landscape between the bakery and the university.

Now I can see the bakery as a new start but, while 30 years later I found myself just down the road presenting lectures and leading seminars about inclusion in education which drew in turn upon my experience as a specialist advisor working with children and their teachers to minimise and avoid exclusion from mainstream schools, I could never have imagined this on the Friday afternoon at the beginning of September 1975, when I took the bus to the bread factory at the edge of town for the fifteen minute job interview. I was unemployed with no qualifications and no references having been expelled from school. I started work in the confectionary department the following Monday. I worked there for three years.

It was another place where you could not see through the windows except in the canteen and I often had that old feeling when I saw the bus go by at dinner time: life going on without me – feeling both forgotten about and controlled, or even 'owned' by someone else. It wasn't an old building but it was an old style factory design you don't see much now. We changed into white trousers and shirts at ground level and then descended down a stairwell into a huge, noisy hangar where three industrial bread plants thumped out loaf after loaf all day and night. Beyond this was the confectionary area where I worked: a series of smaller mixers, belts and ovens for the production of rolls, buns and cakes of all kinds. At the far end of the hangar was a loading area where the food was dispatched by vans to shops around the region. Confectionary was less mechanised than bread so more people were needed to pipe icing, sprinkle sugar and put sausage rolls onto baking trays. Lots of women worked in confectionary and it was regarded as women's work by the big tough guys on bread. I felt the same way. This added to my feeling of failure about working there in the first place. This wasn't what I had in mind. I didn't know what I did have in mind but it wasn't this subterranean, semi-nocturnal, hot, hard, boring and yet rather feminine life of confectionary in the bakery/factory.

It all seemed like a long way from Emmett Grogan and San Francisco although that story was already history as the spirit of the sixties seemed to finally give way to the harsher less generous seventies and Grogan himself was found dead at 35 on the New York subway. I'd found another dead hero in Lenny Bruce by then. The

CHAPTER 5

film and book biographies of Bruce offered another self-indulgent, self-destructive and yet politically active icon who also moved 'suspiciously between underground and underworld'. Through Bruce I found out about jazz and made the connection between the Beats of the fifties and the Hippies of the sixties. I read lots of books and wrote poems that only I read and I started keeping a diary. I spent most of my money on beer for a while but things were changing there too. On the first day at the bakery I met the person who became my wife. We worked on the shortbreads together, sharing the job as we shared our lives for 20 years. She put the cherries on while I sprinkled the sugar and then we swapped around. We went out together a few times and then fell out for a year or so before getting back together before we both left the bakery in 1978. We started living together in 1980 and got married in 1981. Our sons were born in 1984 and 1986 and we were divorced in 1996.

I kept in touch with my 2nd year form tutor from school. I would go to his house to see him and his family two or three times a year and we would talk about what we had been reading. He lent me books and gave me leaflets about communism and the history of socialism and encouraged me to be active and join the communist party which I resisted doing for a few years. I went to some of the meetings but it felt very serious and had the feeling of people trying to control me again.

Drinking and smoking were very much part of my social life when I worked at the bakery. Going to the pub after work and heavy drinking at the weekend was an important part of my life for a few years. Things started to change when I took up boxing again. One of the cleaners at the bakery ran the local boxing club and I went along for training and sparing. It soon became clear that I was not very good at this level and I avoided competition after a while. I enjoyed getting fit, gave up smoking, cut down on drinking and started running on a regular basis. I stopped going to the boxing club when I took a job in the centre of town but I never did stop running.

In the summer students from the university would come to work at the bakery. I worked with an English undergraduate called John who was just a little older than me. We talked about America a lot. I think he was surprised by how much I knew and I was surprised by what seemed like his easy life and limitless opportunities: "I might teach when I finish or may travel for a while," he told me once. We argued on one occasion when I felt he was not working very hard and he said "you have to remember that this is your life Mick, but it's just a summer job for me." It was the truth of what he said that hurt.

I got back in touch with formal education for a while when I started an apprenticeship as a baker in 1977. One of my supervisors told me that I 'came out as a moron in the test results' but he thought I had potential and recommended me anyway. I went to the technical college one day a week in term time. It was good to be out of the factory and I learnt about making bread and cakes by hand, but by then I had decided to move on and I took a job in a large chain carpet shop as a store assistant when they opened a shop in town. It felt less cut off from 'real life' than school or the bakery. Customers and delivery drivers came and went. We used to go out to help to deliver and fit carpets. It was manual, fairly heavy work. I worked at that shop for six years and then at another in the same chain in a nearby town for two more years as warehouse manager. Those eight years between 19 and 27 were a time of growth and change and key events for me: buying a flat, getting married, having children, learning to drive and being promoted. I became active in the union and local politics, read a lot and kept writing poems which only I read.

I applied without success for a job in sales a few times and began to realise that I was already near the limits of where I was going in carpet retail. I also realised that I wanted more than money from my work. I am still not sure where that realisation came from. My parents had been nurses but I don't recall consciously wanting a vocation or even wanting to help other people. I did want more control over my own life. I wanted to be recognised and valued as an individual. I used to feel that as long as some body was unloading the lorry or rolling and cutting the carpets it didn't matter to anyone else whether it was me or not. I wanted a job where it mattered that it was me. I wanted a profession but had no idea which one.

I joined a running club in 1982 when I was 23. There were lots of mainly younger, usually faster athletes who I used to train with and they were going somewhere in their lives as well as on the track. I remember thinking very clearly that I was being left behind in more ways than one as they pulled away from me down the track one Tuesday evening. They were going to universities or taking jobs I'd never heard of or travelling abroad. It was up to me to get fit and catch up and I now thought I just might be able to. I never did catch up with most of them on the track of course (one of them was an Olympic gold medallist and world record holder) but I did enrol to do two 'O' levels at evening class in 1984.

I had rising confidence and motivation by then. My wife was expecting our first child. When I think of all the people who have influenced the direction of my education and life from my parents to my teachers to my partners, friends and students I realise that my eldest son brought about the most change in me and my life, even before he arrived. I was also ready to communicate and I wanted someone to read what I wrote. I had begun to show Mr Sacks the odd poem again and I talked about poetry and writing with a new friend I made through running. He seemed to take me seriously and shared some of the things he had written with me. The weekly writing tasks on the English and History 'O' level courses gave me the opportunity to write for an audience that I now welcomed. I used to go to the college after work and seemed to soak it up like a sponge. I got 'A' grades the following summer and then good 'A' levels a year later.

When I couldn't stand the warehouse anymore I took a job as a milkman for nearly a year and then as a lorry driver but I hated both jobs. The work itself was not enough anymore and doing well at college made me feel that I could do something more interesting. When I sat down and worked out the money in 1987 I realised that if I divided the local authority grant up over 36 polytechnic term-time weeks and did driving and labouring work in the holidays we would actually be better off than if I stayed in full-time low-paid jobs. Even with two children, it didn't really feel like a big risk as I thought I could always go back to that sort of work when I finished the degree in humanities at the polytechnic if I had to.

CHAPTER 5

THE INTERPRETATION AND REPRESENTATION OF SELF-NARRATIVES

This chapter is organised into three themed sections that represent the data through a narrative analysis based upon Sartre's progressive-regressive method (1963) and Denzin's critical interpretive framework (1997, 2001). This is consistent with the analytic autoethnographic framework of methodology adopted from Anderson (2006) in that it aims to examine the conceptual structures which inform the self-narratives, allows the reader to consider how the cultural practices connected to structural formations are experienced by interacting individuals, and offers 'insight into some broader set of social phenomena than those offered by the data themselves' (Anderson, 2006 p387). This is not meant to produce the 'undebatable conclusions' referred to by Ellis and Bochner (2000 p744) but to contribute to what Anderson describes as 'the spiralling refinement, elaboration, extension and revision of theoretical understanding' (2006 p387).

I take this approach to analytic interpretation in an effort to provide interpretations that are 'dialogic, thick and multivoiced' (Denzin, 2001 p133) from the participants' points of view as collected throughout our writing and interviews. The narrative analysis presented in this chapter represents a dialogue between the observer and the observed that foregrounds the articulated interpretations of the participants themselves. It is their own understanding of the significance and consequences of the events and decisions they describe that matters here. This offers thick descriptions that report meanings and intentions and opens the way for interpretations that take the reader to the heart of the stories being told.

Using the Progressive/Regressive Method

By using the progressive/regressive method in the reading and interpretation of the gathered material I was able to situate and to understand the data within a given historical moment without forcing an externally derived theory into the reading of these self-narratives. To recap: the terms 'progressive' and 'regressive' refer to the temporal forward and backward direction of the process of interpretation. When considering the interview transcripts and stories I looked forward to the conclusion of a number of experiences and acts remembered and recorded in the data such as the way Jan's decision to move into teacher education led to her developing new understandings of higher education and the distinct role of the teacher educator. For Jan this led in turn to what she sees as a successful and largely happy career in ITE. I then read regressively back from, for example, that same decision of Jan's towards the historical, cultural and biographical circumstances that informed those experiences and acts, such as Jan's feelings about literacy and literature coming into conflict with the national literacy strategy she was required to teach in school, causing her to feel disillusioned and contributing towards that decision. Jan's narrative on the origins and development of her feelings and beliefs about stories, literacy and teaching take on a new significance in this context. Experiences are placed in time and space illuminating the unique features of our lives while revealing commonalities that we share with each other. Peter's decision to leave his ITE course as a student can be traced forwards, interestingly, to his position as a tutor in ITE. The connections he articulates between his role there and his own career experiences illuminate how his approach to his work, his working pedagogy, has been influenced by that earlier decision and action which he now sees as a turning point moment. Moving back through the data I was able to consider Peter's perceptions of the era and the circumstances that led to this decision and action, through what he has said and written about his own education, early career and family. Sartre argued that each of us is a universal singular, 'universalising in our singularity the crises and experiences of our epoch' (Sartre, 1981, p.ix).

I use a great deal of direct quotation in order to reveal the complexity of the patterns in these stories. The memories and the experiences collected are synthesised and organised into these three sections of narrative analysis rather than an analysis of the narratives (Polkinghorne, 1995), beginning at the 'end' of the story with our experiences of being teacher educators.

ON BEING A TEACHER EDUCATOR

In this section the participants' experiences and perceptions of working in teacher education are presented as a way of illuminating this particular 'culture in practice' (Fiske, 1999 p195). A number of common issues about the role of the university based teacher educator are highlighted here including the significant departure from school teaching, struggles of induction into teacher education, and the challenges and rewards of working in this area of higher education. The central themes arising from the data on being a teacher educator concerning rewards and challenges, difficulties and dilemmas that teacher educators face in carrying out our role and practising what we teach are the particular focus of the subsections below.

I begin with the 'now' of the narrative through the situation we were in as teacher educators when the narratives were written and collected.

> **Data referencing key:**
> (Name.s (story). **or** i (interview). Page number)
> e.g: (Brian.s.2) or (Kay.i.6)

A New Path to the Waterfall

My problem was one of losing confidence and my sense of authenticity:

> While I had felt like part of the problem in the education system to some extent as a school teacher and as an advisor I always felt that I was contributing something positive as well; something the children would benefit from at some time (Mike.s.19).

I felt that less and less during my time as a teacher educator. I needed a new strategy. I sought a new understanding to make the job sustainable and worthwhile,

CHAPTER 5

what Raymond Carver called 'a new path to the waterfall' (Carver, 1989). I could not be simply a teacher, in the way I understood it, anymore.

Jan identified the diminishing returns of recent and relevant experience as a school teacher within the planned obsolescence of seeing her professional credit slip away when she became a teacher educator:

> You have the skills and experience as a teacher…which are highly valued in teacher education, more than other areas really in HE because it's vocational. People who have been working in classrooms recently often have a lot of cachet, lot of status. Sometimes it's the people who have been in the schools of education the longest who begin to lose confidence when it comes to teaching about classroom practice. I know my own confidence in terms of being able to teach teachers about teaching has slipped away a bit, the longer I've been away from the classroom. Which is one of the reasons I like to get back there (supervising students) (Jan.i.7).

It seems that the 'cachet' of our recent and relevant experience as teachers, the very reason we may have got our jobs as teacher educators in the first place, began to lose its value the moment we started the job:

> All you've got and it matters, is your experience, that's what gives you your credibility, only it loses its value fast because schools change all the time. After a year your career's worth of experience is worth less than it was. Schools have changed so much since I came into Higher Education in '94. So you have to replace it with something, build a new sort of portfolio or you find your confidence slipping away (Sian.i.17).

Relying too heavily on a falling currency of experience, my confidence certainly slipped away over the three years I worked as a teacher educator. The place where I had succeeded as an undergraduate and as a PGCE student became a site of confusion, anxiety and what I felt was failure as I struggled to find or adapt a new pedagogy for myself in ITE. Sian recognises that:

> The thing about Higher Education is that nobody does any training. You get the job because you're good at teaching and managing in schools like me…You earn your stripes and maybe do some study…part time MAs and a specialism, and then you get the job at university. But no one teaches you how to teach adults. No one tells you anything about HE so you make it up as you go along the way (Sian.i.16).

While I always knew that teaching adults would differ from school teaching I didn't realise that it is actually a completely different sort of job. I felt de-skilled in a number of ways and wondered about the worth and value of what I was doing. I was unable to articulate a new understanding of the role I had taken on. A sense of loss rather than development ensued. After 13 years, I couldn't easily accept that I had stopped being a teacher in the way I understood it. When I was forced to face up to it I felt bereft: exposed and vulnerable within an unfamiliar and what seemed at times hostile, professional landscape without the protection and tools of a secure professional identity.

The other participants however did develop new professional identities. For Jan this has been about:

> ... recognising that we have a different role here. It is a different sort of job. We make a different contribution to the education of teachers (Jan.i.7).

> A contribution of a different kind...reflection, analysing, understanding the wider context. That is higher education but not as we know it (Jan.i.7).

While I came to see my move into ITE as an end to my school teaching career and was ambivalent about my new role, Jan came to recognise her new role as a continuation of her teaching career even if it was a radical change of direction.

Sian's accounts concur with many of these points and she also describes the differences between institutions and perhaps eras of practice through her experiences within her first and her current appointments in teacher education:

> It was all much more about practice at Swan Hill and I was straight from (teaching in) school. I got into the pattern which was sort of expected where I modelled a lot of technique, demonstrated how to teach class, plan, assess, manage. There wasn't much focus on reflection or finding your own way (Sian.i.16).

The individual nature of the experience of working in Higher Education where few lecturers share the same 'portfolio' or timetable in teacher education can add to feelings of detachment as expressed in the interviews and stories. Sometimes colleagues come together to plan modules and sessions. They usually lecture or tutor students on their own and then go off to meet, plan and teach in different configurations and teams. As Jan puts it:

> We all end up doing different things overall which is really good in some ways but it means you don't get that thing where you sit down at the end of the day because our days end at different times or we work on different days. I might be in school while Kerry is teaching here all day. I might not see her for a month although we do try to meet in our module teams most weeks. We don't all go to the pub on Friday or have lunch together (Jan.i.13).

If the system separates teacher educators physically, different beliefs about what they should and should not be doing can also be divisive:

> Some people they just run the same old stuff out year after year and it sort of works. There's still some things that are timeless I suppose but I think that's why so many teaching students think their lecturers are out of touch. They are! (Sian.i.13).

CHAPTER 5

Brian sees some of the divisions more positively:

> There is a tendency at our place to stick with your subject area. I think that's Ok as subject knowledge is key in teaching and in teacher training in my view. We fight our own corner. Make sure that our subject is properly represented on the courses (Brian.i.15).

Similar allegiances may be formed around subject areas within different schools of education. Jan named 'English' rather than education as her subject and Brian identifies his expertise as being in maths rather than the skills of teaching. Sian felt, as I did that colleagues wedded to subject areas could 'stitch you up' as she puts it (Sian.s.4).

Peter and Kay had different perspectives on this:

> You have to look after yourself in teacher education. People stick in their subject silos when it suits them but even then the system encourages us to turn on each other. One person gains while another loses. It's all very individual (Peter.i.14).

> I've managed to avoid most of the conflict. I'm a sort of mini subject area on my own, one that nobody else really wants to do, so people tend to leave me alone (Kay.i.12).

Whereas Jan identified with some of the feelings that I experienced:

> I certainly felt like that; isolated sometimes and sometimes in competition. You know if you don't take on a module or whatever then someone else will have to and vice versa. What the others won't do you might have to (Jan.i.13).

Rewards

Like Sian, much of Jackie's work is no longer in Initial Teacher Education. They both research and write as much as they work directly with students and most of Jackie's students are already teachers taking MAs or Doctorates in Education. She finds the intellectual stimulation of post-graduate work most rewarding:

> My classroom experience is very limited but I have learnt a lot about research in educational settings. I still do some ITE but I'm mainly working with post-grads who are either teachers or teacher educators themselves. I can't really offer any direct practical advice on classroom teaching, and that's not really my role, but the feedback I get from students often says that my input has helped them to understand and develop their practice (Jackie.i.14)

This was an aspect I too found rewarding. I taught and supervised on the MA education course at the university. It was the time I felt more like an educator than a trainer. Peter felt the standard of teaching and learning was 'higher' in Further Education (FE), where most students are between 16 and 19 years old, than it was in Initial Teacher Education (post 19 year olds):

It was a real step back I can tell you. I thought 'Higher than what?' (Peter.i.14).

But Peter found the working conditions at the university preferable to FE. His experience of working with adults meant that he had a familiarity that other participants lacked when we began in ITE. The vocational aspects of FE fed into teacher education:

> You can't forget that the students are preparing to do a job with everything that entails. This is an important aspect of the work. I always had to keep this in mind working in FE so I didn't find it difficult when I started in ITE ... Some people say it dominates too much but I think it should to some extent. We want the students to be successful, educated, teachers which means being employed as teachers (Peter.i.15).

Kay agrees and doesn't see anything narrow about vocational education:

> That's where the two come together; in the classroom. Teachers need a sound understanding of how people learn and which teaching strategies and techniques work best but what is the point of knowing all these things if you can't apply it in the classroom? I measure our success as a school (of education) by how the students get on as teachers in the short, medium and longer term (Kay.i.15).

Seeing students become teachers is clearly one of the rewards of teacher education:

> I love that feeling of going into a school to see a student and either the teacher they are working with or another teacher in the school used to be your student. Even if you didn't know them very well, I always feel as though I've played my part in that, made a contribution (Jackie.i.15)

Challenges

One of the things that may have made it difficult for me to adopt a new professional identity in ITE is that it sits in an ambiguous position in some ways. The narratives of this data show that old dualities persist in our thinking when considering whether we are lecturers in the study of education or teacher trainers.

Sometimes there is pressure to be more academic. This can come from colleagues, senior management, or other departments:

> Education is regarded as the slow lane at the university where I work. If you get into discussion with colleagues from other schools they often don't know what we do. 'Teacher training' is the usual description from the outside. The implication is that education is solely about training students who want to be teachers (Jackie.i.16).

Peter's Dean of Faculty is disappointed with the school of education's contributions to the Research Assessment Exercise and:

CHAPTER 5

> The vice chancellor thinks we are very conventional as he puts it from time to time. We are seen as pedestrian and conforming. It's partly because we have to dance to the external tunes of Ofsted and the TDA. They're our real bosses as far as the management are concerned (Peter.i.15).

Peter has a point. The Training and Development Agency provide funding to the university for training teachers and so the term 'teacher training provider' is not too far off the mark. It could be seen as part of a franchise where there is an illusion of independence, autonomy and academic freedom.

Brian has no such illusions and doesn't see this as a bad thing:

> We talk a lot about ideas. Different sorts of approaches, what the students need etc. But in the end we are like school teachers – we have to teach a syllabus, we have to follow a curriculum and to some extent we have to use certain methods (Brian.s.2).

Jan saw some of the problems and pressures that she had felt in schools pursue her into ITE during the 1990s:

> Lots of the changes that happened in schools in the 80s and 90s seemed to filter through into teacher education especially since 4/98, the notorious memo ... Over the next 18 months or so things really turned on their head. We re-wrote the course and I found myself teaching the teachers to teach the literacy hour which I ran away from (Jan.i.8).

Academic freedom seems far away for someone who is teaching a method and a philosophy they profoundly disagree with. In the past there had been more flexibility:

> There were always things that teacher educators thought we did too much of or not enough of. Things we thought were questionable or had doubts about their worth. We all had to do that as teachers in school. It's part of the job. The difference with the new legislation in the 80s and 90s was that it actually required, legally required teachers to follow methods that they disagreed with (Sian.s.4).

This was even more the case in schools of education where teacher educators were required to train students for a system and method they often professed to oppose and which went against their readings of educational research.

For teacher educators like Jan independence of both content and method has been further constrained in a similar way to schools:

> We've got a bit more flexibility in some ways. We can interpret things but it's all so much tighter than it used to be and we always have Ofsted. Ofsted is always with us (looking towards the sky) ... You can't go off and do your own thing. The students have to meet very particular standards in very particular ways (Jan.i.12).

To ignore or challenge these particular standards would be to let the students down in Jan's view:

> It would be like not teaching the GCSE syllabus to 16year olds who were taking the exams. You have to accept it. It's not like being an academic in that way (Jan.i.12).

Practising What We Teach

The external standards that provide many of the preconditions of practice for teacher educators strongly influence the conceptions they carry with them of their own work and provide a site of potential tension with what they believe and feel about teaching and the education of teachers. The data presented in this book: my own narrative, the interviews conducted with the six other teacher educators and the short self-narratives written by five of them about their work as teacher educators provides illumination and insight into what we think about our jobs and our roles and why we think and feel that way. The 'biographical perspective' I have taken assumes that the professional behaviour of teacher educators is largely determined by experiences from the past and expectations of the future.

Kelchtermans (1993) provides a useful framework in tracing this biographical perspective in the study of teachers, acknowledging the importance of experience in the formation of their personal opinions and implicit theories about education. The centrality of life experience and personal background as determinants of teachers' thinking and professional behaviour is also demonstrated by research of teacher socialisation and the focus upon critical incidents and phases in teachers' career stories (Goodson 1992, 2003; Munro, 1998; Sikes et al., 1985). One common and critical incident for the participants in this study is the move we made into teacher education from teaching in schools or colleges. This can be seen as the end of our school teaching careers even if it also offered a new beginning.

It is important to return here to the links between the personal and the public and to re-emphasise the importance of context, taking account of the structural, cultural and organisational context in which teacher-educators work while considering individual development. The professional biography remains a result of a dialectical relationship between a person and their professional environment. The new circumstances provided by, for example, new curricula, legislation or policy causes things to be re-configured with aspects of belief and 'feeling' being adapted and reformulated.

As teacher educators we have become closely aware of our restricted and contrived positions at different points and attempted in different ways to improve our teaching and the learning of our students in an effort to somehow 'square the circle' by practising what we teach. As such we find ourselves in ambivalent situations. Gaps appear between what we believe and what we do in our work. These are the professional dilemmas of teacher educators: the gap between practice espoused and practised. The response is to attempt to establish a personal pedagogy of teacher education, and in so doing teacher educators are faced with a number of dilemmas. The following subsections identify some of the dilemmas that arose in the data and the ways in which we seven teacher educators deal with and attempt to deal with them informed by our own histories. The professional dilemmas that teacher educators recognise and resolve reveal how they succeed in connecting their own views on teaching, including their views on teaching how to teach, to their actual teaching. By gauging these professional dilemmas and linking this with individual experiences we can understand what governs the relationship between conceptions and beliefs about teaching and teaching itself for university based teacher educators.

Ambiguous Roles

The central dilemma for me during my first phase in teacher education was linked to my views on pedagogy and a feeling that I was not teaching in a way I believed in, but the focus of anxiety was often more upon my feelings about working relationships with colleagues. Management structures were often semi-formal in that apart from the head of school there were no other line managers or heads of department as such. Course leaders, subject co-ordinators and phase and activity co-ordinators such as 'partnership co-ordinator' or 'ITE co-ordinator' abound especially in the larger schools of education. But these are voluntary positions to some extent. Appointments made without application or interview and often as in my case against the wishes of the appointee after some resistance. I had tried to avoid becoming subject co-ordinator after only a year in ITE but to no avail. It seemed that I was the right person in the wrong place at the wrong time depending on how you looked at it. To read forward from my decision to accept the role brings me to the perspective that I now had a management role to perform with no experience of management or administration outside of my own classroom experience which felt like responsibility without power. It was my inability to resolve these feelings that led to my resignation the following year.

I was profoundly uncomfortable about organising the work of my colleagues, assigning courses and modules to staff and organising teaching schedules and timetables. Not only did it contradict many of my own beliefs and concerns about workers being positioned so as to exploit each other, it also made me feel personally vulnerable to criticisms of betrayal and being personally ambitious. I did not want to be unpopular. In fact I encountered very little direct criticism as I grappled with the role. People sometimes refused to do things or challenged my decisions, sometimes going over my head to get things changed, but rarely were any direct criticisms made of me. I was busy making those criticisms of myself, feeling like a turncoat in some ways even if others did not see me that way. The origins of these feelings can be identified by reading back through my own narrative along with, more surprisingly to me, the origins of the feelings that contributed towards me reluctantly taking on the role in the first place, such as feelings of insecurity, the need for approval and attention, a desire for and a fear of responsibility.

The other participants experienced similar situations although the nomenclature varied between institutions. The titles of such jobs are interchangeable as Peter discovered at his institution:

> At one time we were co-ordinators and then you would hear 'subject leader' or 'head of subject' being knocked about. There are actually a lot of different meanings in those phrases and titles. It revealed how people saw themselves in my view (Peter.i.16).

Posts like these, if posts are what they are, do not in themselves increase salary:

> People do them for years for nothing. They're so lumpen in schools of education, so quick to take responsibility and boss other people around. You get it in schools of course. Jumped up heads of department and deputy heads but at least they get paid for it, and everyone can apply - in theory at least (Brian.i.14).

Sian is a course leader. The question of whether the job carried any real authority as well as responsibility and whether the post was remunerated was solved for her when she was made principal lecturer:

> It's not strictly linked to the post but I made a good case when I applied. Running the course is a big responsibility so it was hard for our head to say no. I felt as though the promotion made the course leadership into a real job that was being properly recognised and believe me I earn that extra money (Sian.s.4).

Jan has managed to avoid taking on too much and prefers to put her energy into teaching and supervising students:

> I was lucky. Our department is fairly big and full of people who just love telling other people what to do. I've got some administrative responsibilities but I've avoided the co-ordinator/course leader trap (Jan.s.4).

But Jackie enjoys being a course leader:

> I think people agonise too much about all that. Someone has to co-ordinate things. I never felt any animosity towards others who led teams, courses or subject areas. I was actually grateful to them for their hard work in many ways. I do a good job here as well and it saves the others from doing it. There will always be some disagreement, but I never meant it personally in the past and I don't take it personally now that I'm a course leader (Jackie.i.15).

Keeping Up

The need to build on one's own professionalism in ITE, which often includes taking on administrative and management roles, opens the way for a series of

CHAPTER 5

dilemmas for teacher educators. Maintaining motivation and creative energy with all the external demands and dealing with pressure and innovation are typical in this group. My own dissonance when the role of subject co-ordinator seemed to take all my time and energy while I was still learning the ITE ropes might be an example of this, as is Peter's situation as ICT subject co-ordinator in a school of education:

> For a long time I felt I had to keep up with everything in ICT and everything in secondary and everything in post compulsory education. I found myself keeping up with everything and not being able to do anything. I was on the verge of another breakdown. I could have been the best informed basket case in Britain (Peter.i.16).

The desire to improve our work as teacher educators brings further challenges such as the need to 'stay fresh', avoiding too much routine and how to apply new knowledge and understanding in our work. The need to focus on excellence and competencies in teaching while recognising the value of different approaches and individual strengths is a site of a number of dilemmas. Sian's barely concealed contempt for those colleagues who repeat the same things year after year (Sian.i.13) reveals her own concerns and the need to stay fresh and keep her work relevant and interesting for herself as well as the students.

Supporting Students, Ourselves and Each Other

Responsibilities of guidance and mentorship of students brings forth questions concerning our own abilities to be good mentors and guides although only I seemed to have real doubts about my own abilities here. All of the other participants felt that it was an issue of time and resources. As Brian put it:

> I'm happy to support students although it's not my job to counsel them or provide therapy. From a teaching and professional point of view I want to guide and mentor them when I can but I don't really get to see them often enough (Brian.i.16).

The tension between being part of a team and taking an individual approach surfaces in perceived dilemmas such as the need to have good relationships with teachers in schools, working closely with school-based mentors, coping with workload and stress and the needs and demands of colleagues in teams.

Beliefs about teaching itself are put under stress when teacher educators consider the experiences and needs of students:

> I'm a constructivist, social constructivist and I would like to recommend that all student teachers should learn, know about, and teach using methods based upon these ideas, but they can't jump straight into the deep end. It took me many years and lots of further study before I could call myself a

constructivist teacher. I was much more of a conservative teacher for years (Jackie.i.16).

Some of us felt torn between authoritative and more permissive styles of teaching:

> I would like to be more flexible, more open, and more collaborative but I have to admit that, depending on the students, authoritative and teacher – focussed teaching often works better (Peter.s.3).

This leads on to further questions of whether we should be guiding students or providing more direct mentorship:

> My preference is to guide students and let competencies develop gradually as they need to be autonomous professionals at some point. But my students have always expected me to tell them what to do. They take any suggestion as gospel and implement it straight away (Sian.s.4).

Issues of accountability trouble some participants here:

> I am expected to account for my students' achievement, my part in it anyway, but I don't have the power or the autonomy to change what they learn and how they learn it (Brian.s.3).

> One of the problems remains the fact that we are not clear and agreed on what we think a successful student is at the end of our ITE courses apart from being able to get a job and teach class. Differences in what we believe schools are for and what teachers are about influence our perspectives (Jackie.i.17).

Relationships with students and whether these should be formal or more flexible vary in this group but all are agreed on the tensions between the responsibilities of timetabled teaching and research and writing.

ON BEING A TEACHER

This section examines the memories of the experience of being a teacher as they emerged in my own and the other narratives. Here the particular experiences of teaching children and adolescents in schools and colleges is represented and discussed in an attempt to suggest ways in which we have identified these experiences as influencing our beliefs and our pedagogies concerning teacher education. The sub-sections here represent the sites and contexts of teaching that can be identified within the interviews and stories.

It took me a long time to decide to be a teacher. While I recognise in my narrative that the process may have begun back in primary school with Mr Marley, I was never conscious of this during my time at school and if someone had suggested the possibility in my teens I would have rejected the idea out of hand along with most other people. This had as much to do with self-confidence and low self-esteem as it did with my own ambivalence towards schools. I just didn't see myself that way. But as the story states, I became a primary school teacher in 1991 at the age of 31 and taught children in a number of settings until 2004. Here I want

CHAPTER 5

to look at my perceptions of how working as a teacher for those 13 years influenced and shaped what I came to understand and believe about schools, teachers and learners and how this has influenced my pedagogy as a teacher educator. As in the previous section the neighbouring narratives of the other participants are used alongside and intertwined with my own at relevant intersections where commonalities and points of departure can be explored in an attempt to situate this part of the story.

Getting There

I had come to see myself in a different way before I signed up for the PGCE. I had crossed some sort of zone of proximal development (Vygotsky, 1978) with the intellectual scaffolding of the BA (Hons) and there was no going back. The study and the expectation of graduation expanded my possibilities in my own mind as the experience of being a parent and visiting schools put me back in touch with primary education and provided me with a new perspective on how they had changed:

> I didn't have to leave my son in the playground on his first day and he seemed much happier at school than I had been (Mike.s.15).

The tale goes on to cite the book launching event which took place at the same school where I was struck by the children's enthusiasm and good will:

> It was an enjoyable and friendly occasion. I think it put teaching back at the forefront of my mind as a possibility and made me see it beyond my own experience as a pupil (Mike.s.16).

It was during my PGCE year that I knew that I wanted to be a teacher and that I began to really believe I could do it. Jackie did not have to overcome such negative memories or doubts about her own ability but after working in schools in Africa and India she never felt especially committed to teaching in schools in England.

> I thought it was a good idea. Sensible to get a job that I could do if I needed to ... soon into the PGCE, certainly after my first teaching practice, I knew that I wasn't going to be doing it for very long and definitely not for the rest of my career (Jackie.i.7).

She did work in a primary school for three years but feels that she was never very settled and found that it provided neither the sense of adventure nor the feeling of worthwhile value that she gained from her overseas efforts. There was also a lack of intellectual stimulation and engagement as far as Jackie was concerned:

> I found it increasingly dull from a personal point of view. I liked the children and the staff. I didn't have any problems. In some ways it was all rather easy. Probably too easy when I look back (Jackie.i.8).

Whereas, at the age of 31 on qualification, I thought it might be a job for the rest of my working life. I had mixed feelings about this.

Sian had already decided that she wanted one day to work in teacher education before she qualified as a teacher although it was 15 years before she took up such a post in a university:

> I had it in mind from time to time. It was sort of in the background like something I might work towards and do in the future. I knew ... I could cut it. I knew I had the academic skills but I wasn't in any hurry. I was alright in school (Sian.i.14).

Making 'connections between the sort of community politics and activities I was involved with, a developing philosophy of personal growth and change leading to social change and working in school' (Mike.s.16) provided an emerging working narrative for me which has remained central to my own belief and informed my practice. This was a driving force of sorts that continued to challenge and motivate me throughout my time as a school teacher. It was a resource for facing difficult times and changes and then later sometimes a source of disappointment and pain. While wanting to change things can stimulate and motivate not being able to can lead to frustration and a growing sense of isolation. I felt personally empowered by this understanding but professionally undermined by what I saw as restrictive structures that were exerting pressures and tensions upon my ability to teach in the way I wanted to. It seemed as though so much of the reform that was taking place in schools was going against what I thought I believed in and the emerging culture of performativity (Ball 2003) was making me into someone I didn't want to be.

Kay remembers only ever wanting to be a teacher. Her memory of starting to teach for a living is enviably uncomplicated:

> K: It was as though someone was going to pay me for doing something that I would have been quite happy to do in my own time. I'd been teaching in one way or another remember, on a voluntary basis, since I was a young girl
> M: Were you nervous when you started?
> K: Hmm more excited than nervous really. I felt very optimistic. Not frightened, not at all frightened. Maybe a bit worried about whether I'd know all I needed to know but more than competent to make a start (Kay.i.13).

Concerns over competences to teach and the need to control the class were concerns that arose even for Jan who had wanted to be a teacher since she was 14:

> I always wanted to work primary – those grumpy (secondary) kids remember? (Jan.i.3).

Peter recognises that his anxiety that he was being asked to exert too much control over the children and to act as a representative of many traditional values that he opposed undermined his progress as a student teacher:

> At the (placement) school they went on and on about keeping 'them' under control. The children. It was a sort of 'don't smile until Christmas' approach.

CHAPTER 5

'If you get too friendly they'll walk all over you'. Oh there was some truth in all that I suppose. The battle lines had been drawn up long before I got there of course but I didn't want to be part of that (Peter.i.14)

Brian hints at settling for second best in becoming a teacher to some extent:

B: It suited me. It was the right thing to do at the time. I wasn't going to make a living as a musician and I did want to make a contribution to society, to the community.
M: So no regrets?
B: It was the right thing to do at the time.

Being There

Whether we had wanted to be teachers since childhood like Kay and Jan, came to the idea through various necessities as with Brian, Sian and me, or never really embraced it like Jackie and Peter we all note the transformative nature of being a teacher in our narrative recounting. We agree that teaching changes people in all sorts of ways and demonstrate in our narratives how it has shaped our identities.

Kay believes she became the person she wanted to be and that being a teacher facilitated this. Her optimistic perspective infuses her interview and story narrative with a positive retrospective glow of ambition met and aims achieved during her career as a teacher.

I state clearly that: 'I think I became a good teacher' but I go on to state the concern that:

I never did completely get rid of the feeling that someone might come into the classroom and ask me what I was doing there and tell me to leave (Mike.s.17).

Jan does not share a memory of that kind but she did feel something like that later in her career when:

I was becoming frustrated with primary teaching. It seemed to be more restrictive than it had been ... literacy in particular. It wasn't really what I wanted to do any more...' (Jan.i.6).

While Brian was disappointed with the way his school teaching career ended after 25 years he always felt that he was making a contribution and in some way helping to improve society through education:

You can't change individual people directly of course. They have to do that for themselves. But you can offer something and be a positive influence as a teacher. You can show that you respect them and share what you know about a subject and then help them to learn and show them how to apply that learning in their lives. It's all about application when you get down to it ... You can also offer an example. Some of the lads and the girls that I taught, they did OK. I played my part in that success. I drew on my own experiences as a child, as a learner and as a teacher. I was an example of how it didn't have to be the same old same old for them (Brian.s.2).

Brian sees his role in helping his pupils to aspire to and achieve better things in their lives. To break out of what he sees as the cycles of deprivation and like him, but unlike his brother, escape from some of the negative aspects of their lives and backgrounds.

Perceived failure and struggle in education, be it our own or those close to us becomes a motivating factor for some of us as teachers. Behind even Kay's optimism is the memory of her parents' lack of opportunity:

I got a chance my Mother and Father didn't get and I took it. I wanted to give other people the same opportunities to reach their potential in all sorts of ways (Kay.s.2).

For Sian the opportunity she wanted to provide was as much a way of seeing the world and getting the most out of it as it was about qualifications and jobs. Her teaching was informed by:

... a personal philosophy. I think everyone is capable of being poetic and creating beautiful things thoughts and actions even if they don't want to or they don't know it (Sian.i.9).

S: It's been a sort of bedrock. When I was a teacher I thought that if the pupils could begin to move that way then they had a chance of living fulfilling lives. You know whatever they ended up doing. They could be builders or nurses or secretaries or whatever but they would see things in a bigger way and maybe, probably, they'd want more from their jobs but that's not the main thing. Do you see?

M: Yeah I do. I can see what you mean and that happened did it, lots of times when you were teaching?

S: Transformation? You bet ... they do actually change before your eyes...sometimes I had something to do with that (Sian.i.10).

Jan also remembered the rewards of teaching in school:

There's nothing like teaching children (Jan.i.6)...

I mean you can see the kids learning in front of you. They change before your eyes (Jan.i.17).

And what she sees as a common motivation for all teachers:

Whatever you teach, you know any age or phase here or at school you want your learners to have that 'whoosh' and you want to be part of it (Jan.i.17).

The 'whoosh' or the 'wow' factor certainly motivated me as a teacher. I had found something important to do: 'I felt it mattered and now it did matter, sometimes too

CHAPTER 5

much, that it was me' (Mike.s.18). But like Peter, I began to feel that the system itself made me into a sort of policeman, especially when working with younger children at key stage 1:

> I tried to be fair and kind and gentle. I tried to encourage independence in the children but there was something about the system that put me in a position of control. It was more than making decisions and organising the teaching. I had to exercise control over the children and it bothered me ... Sometimes it felt as though the teachers were planning and trying to control what the children thought as well as what they did (Mike.s.18).

The tension and the contradiction between facilitating learning in open ways and the responsibilities and pressure to control learning in narrow ways with defined and closely specified outcomes has been a career-long issue for some participants:

Jan felt it most keenly when the National Literacy Strategy came into schools:

> That pretty much killed it for me. Although I was teaching lots of subjects, English was my first love. The literacy strategy took all the fun out of it (Jan.i.5).

Brian remembers being constrained by the atmosphere and regime that emerged in the wake of the OFSTED inspections of schools:

> It had a terrible influence on our place. People who had been doing a good job for many years, people like me, came under some pretty nasty pressure to do things differently. Even before we knew OFSTED were coming, our management team were running around with manuals and lists of standards and criteria about what makes a good teacher. I thought 'am I doing a good job or not?' Seems like the answer had always been 'yes' and then it turned into 'no' around that time (Brian.s.2).

Kay felt the pinch of new systems of record-keeping:

> K: Our local authority advisors were obsessed with it. They called it assessment but it wasn't assessment. Our head didn't have the spine to tell them where to go. Nobody's head had the spine to tell them where to go. We had to spend hours filling in forms and ticking boxes about every subject. It meant nothing. Nobody used it. Nobody ever looked at it again.
>
> M: Did you resist that pressure, outwardly, collectively?
>
> K: We, some us argued against it but nobody was listening. The unions were in a bit of a bind. They weren't very strong by the late 80s or early 90s of course and they didn't want to look as though they were against raising standards and accountability. It was a nightmare. No one was listening to us.
>
> M: The teachers?
>
> K: No one seemed to care what the teachers thought about it all (Kay.i.15).

While Peter had by-passed the earlier phases of the growing control over teachers and some of what he had seen as the pressure upon him to control others by dropping out of his QTS course and teaching in post-compulsory education, teaching in a further education college also had its stresses during this era:

> It became more or less compulsory to go to college if you didn't have a job and were under 18. You couldn't get any benefits if you weren't doing something. So we had youngsters there who really didn't want to be there (P.i.12).

As the student numbers increased to meet targets and reduce the unemployment statistics FE college budgets and resources became stretched to the limit:

> We found the classes were much bigger. We had to teach other basic skills subjects sometimes. The odd thing was that I quite liked doing that, and I liked some of the kids who didn't really want to be there. They were more diverse and interesting in some ways (Peter.i.14).

Teaching changed me but not always in the way I wanted it to. I developed a sense of always having to prove myself. So transformation may not always be desirable and certainly cannot be neatly controlled. A growing sense of a lack of authenticity can result. I found myself standing on a thin rug of practice and belief that I found hard to explain or understand which was to be swiftly pulled away as I started work in ITE where a different sort of 'performance' was required.

More Study

Jackie had been bored by three years of teaching to some extent: 'Once the chance of going back to university to do the MA appeared, I jumped at it' (Jackie.i.9). She left teaching to take her MA which focussed upon education in developing countries with an emphasis on post-colonialism and the curriculum. She felt that university teaching and lecturing was the job where she could best use her scholarship, experience and skills.

Brian gained his MA early in his teaching career and came to regard himself as an expert in Mathematics and mathematics teaching. He continues to see himself as an expert in mathematics rather than education. The influence of subject area specialism on ITE practice and pedagogy is understandably strongest for the secondary and FE practitioners among us. Sian, Brian and Peter all recognise that their curriculum subject areas had a strong influence on their memories of teaching and influence upon their development. Brian remains firmly in the mode of maths. Sian enjoyed developing her skills in Science and then later and more extensively in RE, while Peter, feeling secure in his subject knowledge of ICT and his ability to teach it to students seems to have enjoyed developing his understanding more broadly through working with students on basic skills and life-skills modules in FE. Sian's MA was in education; Brian went for pure maths while Peter took ICT and education.

CHAPTER 5

Those with experience of primary practice being myself, Kay, Jan and Jackie were more varied in our views of the influence of curriculum subject areas on our pedagogy. Only Jan expressed a real specialism in terms of curriculum, English being her inspiration and her route in and out of school teaching. She took the MA in Education where she concentrated on elements of language and literacy acquisition while working at the university. Jackie never fell in love with a particular aspect or curriculum area. My own enthusiasm was history but this changed over my years of teaching. I became more interested in the social development and the skills of learning how to learn especially after taking my MA in education, and Kay's primary concerns have been pastoral. We all acknowledge the key role of language.

It may have been boredom, stress or ambition, or it could have been curiosity and genuine academic interest, or it may have been a combination of all of these that made me sign up for the Open University MA in Education while I was a full-time teacher. The idea was to enhance one's practice. My practice was enhanced but so too was my critical thinking and it worked both ways:

> ... this added to my questions. I could see the ways in which pressure and stress as well as values are passed down the line from politicians to children and the part that teachers play in that process. I was able to research, examine and write about this but I never managed to change it within my own situation at key stage 2 or key stage 1 (Mike.s.18).

Sian was less explicit but did indicate in her interview that school teaching had been hard for her at times. For example, when she was talking about her current job:

> I earn a good wage and more importantly, I like what I do. I don't wake up and dread the day ahead ... I mean we get our share of problems (and) pressure but it's nothing like school (Sian.i.4)

Like me, Brian and Peter, Sian took her MA while working full-time as a teacher. For her it was part of a long-term plan to return to University as a lecturer in teacher education: 'It was the thing that made it possible for me. I knew I could work at that level if I needed to' (Sian.s.3).

Moving On

Most of us joined teacher education in stages. We got part-time work as visiting lecturers in schools of education and then when a full-time post came up we were strong candidates. This happened to me, Peter, Sian, Jackie and Kay. Jan and Brian got full time jobs as 'outside candidates' without having first made connections to the schools of education.

Once I started the part-time work as a visiting lecturer I knew where I was heading. I was in a position which I couldn't sustain in my current job and saw the university as a means of escape without returning to the mainstream. I had moved out of the mainstream into working with children identified as having emotional, behavioural and social difficulties which rang a few bells with me to say the least. It took me into a variety of schools. I worked with other adults, other agencies and parents, but I knew I had to get out.

So what was I looking for when I went into Higher Education and Teacher Education?

> It seemed to offer the perfect combination of ideas into practice that I had been struggling with (Mike.s.19).

And what were the others looking for as they began work as teacher educators?

Jan: I saw the job advertised: primary English – teaching teachers, and I thought why not? I'm sure I've got something to offer and it's a way I might be able to have an influence on the way the English is being taught (Jan.i.6).

Sian: I knew it would take some time but I knew I wanted to do this

M: Teach teachers?

Sian: Yeah, work with people who were learning about education and going into or working in education (Sian.i.2).

Kay: I wanted to stay in touch with education and schools. I wanted to make my contribution. After all this time I must have something to offer (Kay.i.14).

Peter: It was the next step for me. I never did work with children in schools and now I felt I was. I wanted to realise my old ambition but stay one step removed. Have my cake and eat it in a way (Peter.i.16).

Jackie: Academic, educational enquiry and research. My own and others. That's a key part of teacher education in my view. That's my niche (Jackie.i.13).

Brian: I wasn't ready to retire. I've got too much to offer. I wanted to stay in the mix ... and I needed the money! (Brian.i.13)

ON BEING A LEARNER

This section examines the memories of the experience of being a learner as they emerged within my narrative and within the interviews with and stories written by the participants as part of the study. The experiences that run through and surface as the narratives intersect within this area reflect how the ways in which we view our experiences of learning have influenced our beliefs about teaching and our work as teacher educators. The following sub-sections represent the relational sites and contexts of learning that can be identified within the interviews and stories.

CHAPTER 5

Families

All of our parents seemed to support the idea of education. Some were active like mine and Jan's while others were more passive in their support:

> They supported it (education) up to a point. Certainly it was a means to an end for them, although they were suspicious of people who might use it to avoid doing a good day's work (Brian. i.1).

> I realise now that education was also a way to entertain yourself before TV. My Dad read lots, usually about wars and soldiers. Education for pleasure. There's a thought. (Sian.s.2).

Jackie's parents were prepared to pay for her education in a private school but she believes this reveals their wish to distance themselves from the process to some extent:

> They wanted me to have what they saw as the best education that they could afford to pay for but they didn't want to be too involved themselves. I sometimes think that people with money try to buy their way out of their children's education like they buy their way out of cleaning their own houses, but there's no doubt that my parents saw a good education at school as the key to a successful life and they were prepared to make sacrifices so that we could have one (Jackie.i.3.).

While he had himself been working full time since the age of 12, Kay's father was:

> ... determined that I and my sister would get the very most out of our opportunities to learn and gain qualifications at school. He thought some of what we learnt there was of no real use to man nor beast as he would put it but he encouraged us to do our best and learn all we could (Kay.i.2).

Scepticism about some of what we were being taught did not seem to make our parents less certain about the need to make the most of our time at school. It was a view we all knew and sometimes shared as children and one that became firmly established in Britain during the 1950s and 1960s. The idea that 'education was the 'route towards a better life'' (Mike.s.3) for individuals and a better society for all has been such a powerful and persuasive position since the 1940s in Britain and is reflected in participants interviews and writing. We are all part of the generations that identified education through school as a means of self-improvement and we all, in different ways, see ourselves as evidence to support this view. A discourse of education and a cultural narrative of self-improvement are revealed here. We are informed by these ideals which can be identified within the Education Act of 1944 to a certain extent. Our stories are shaped by this influence as we play our part in reshaping and reproducing it, initially as learners and then later as teachers and teacher educators.

Siblings offered examples of getting it right or wrong as we engaged with this narrative at school. My brothers had very different experiences which highlighted the contrast of what I saw as success and failure at school and came to understand as contributing to my own fear of failure, rejection and institutional power.

Kay's sister was different from her:

> She never liked school. She has never been able to understand why I wanted to be a teacher. She was bored all the time. But she did alright. She left as soon as she could. She was glad to leave and then she got married quite young and got on with having a family and didn't go out to work. She even hated going into school when her children were young (Kay.i.4).

While Jackie had to cope with her sister's success as head girl:

> I was always in her shadow to some extent. Even after she'd left teachers or the head would mention her in glowing terms. I just had to live with it but it got on my nerves sometimes. I mean she was great, is great, but I didn't always want to be seen as her sister. I wanted to be my own person in my own right. I love my sister but I made sure I went to a different university I can tell you (Jackie.i.4).

Schools

The male participants in this study seemed to hold and express their early memories of starting school in the 1950s and 60s most vividly such as my own from 1964 (Mike.s.3–4) and Peter's from 1968:

> I ran off and hid with a friend while my mother was talking to the teacher. We weren't frightened or upset. Just mucking about. Mum and the teacher were laughing and calling us as though it were a game and we jumped out and the teacher was smiling and said 'go on – in you go' and we both ran into the class. I didn't even kiss my mother goodbye. About an hour later I was ready to go home and then realised she had gone. I spent the rest of the day bawling. (Peter. i.2).

Brian remembers spending his first day at school without talking to anyone but was 'fine the next day'... 'It just seemed familiar and there were other children starting that day who were newer than I was' (Brian.i.2).

Whereas Kay felt:

> ... so pleased to be there. I had been looking forward to it. We used to play schools at home and I had been going to Sunday school and I loved it. I assumed it was going to be a happy and rewarding experience and it largely was. I knew most of the children in my class already of course. The teacher was a bit grumpy but we didn't think that was our fault. Teachers were grumpy in those days (Kay.s.2).

CHAPTER 5

Some participants had few or no memories of their first days in compulsory education. My own strong and negative memories of crying and feeling abandoned in the playground and feeling cut-off from the 'real world' which continued outside the school walls stands out in this particular group, as does the way in which my years of compulsory education ended with expulsion. Getting attention through 'inappropriate' behaviour is not however exclusive to my story. Jan recognises what she now sees as spiteful behaviour towards her sister as 'a way of letting everyone know that I was number one sister, number one kid' (Jan.s.2), but she was rarely in any real trouble at school. None of the other participants remember breaking the rules or being punished and only I seem to have been in trouble with the police during my time at school.

My two brothers represented the polar extremes of educational failure or success for me as a child: the 'backward' school or the technical school. Educational success, even if it came late allowed participants to think about ourselves in different ways. Recognition of earlier success at school is a common theme in these stories and interviews and is often linked to a sort of commitment to learning and a desire to repeat the success and gain attention, recognition and respect:

> I realised that I had made something good that impressed others. As well as a lesson in using and sharing imagination I may also have seen that I could get the attention of the people I cared about in positive ways by doing something good (Mike.s.3).

Brian's memory of a parents' evening when he was ten retains its power:

> Mum was very jovial and happy when they got back and she was saying 'well done Brian top of the class, oh it just gets better and better with you', but Dad, and this is when I knew I was doing well, Dad could hardly speak, he was really moved. I could tell how proud he was. He hugged me really hard, squeezed the life out of me he did, and he hardly ever hugged us, and he just said 'well done son, well done'. It still brings tears to my eyes. (Brian.i.4).

Jackie knew that she was doing well when she was given the end of year prize and made a prefect:

> Mum and Dad said 'well done' and I might have got a present or something but they didn't make a big deal about it. My sister had been head girl so it was sort of expected I think. I must have been very arrogant and over-confident at 15. I don't know what would have happened if I hadn't got the prize or been made a prefect (Jackie.i.5).

Peter found secondary school difficult at times:

> I always had the feeling that my parents were rather disappointed with my results at school. I was pretty miserable and lonely and got very average results although I did get my 'A' levels in the end (Peter.s.1)

Teachers

Although my own parents did not use physical punishment, it was not until my own children were at school that I realised how strange it was that teachers hit children quite regularly at my primary school in the 1960s and that this was not unusual at the time. While the head teacher at my school seems to have used some methods which can now be seen as bullying, all of the participants had memories of what they now perceive as being bullied by teachers in one way or another. Sometimes physically and often through sarcasm and nasty comments:

> She sort of looked at me and sneered and said 'oh you do have a high opinion of yourself don't you?' When I held her stare for a moment her nostrils sort of flared and she said, 'Well we will have to ask your mother to make her way down from Tolby Street for a quiet word or two I think'. I knew what she was saying, and so did everyone else. (Sian.s.3).

Sian's own memories of Tolby Street inform her view of what the teacher was saying to her when she was twelve. She remembers it herself as a place to escape from and education was her route. The memory of being made to feel uncomfortable in one way or another by teachers is a common theme. Participants indicate that this influenced them as both teachers of children and as lecturers of students preparing to teach.

> Teachers can't take their own troubles out on the children. I was always very careful about that myself. I remember teachers who blew their top when I was a kid. You can't respect people like that. It's not easy sometimes. You find yourself feeling angry for what seems like no reason. That's when you have to take a deep breath and have a number of strategies in place. I always tell my students that they need to prepare for feeling angry but never, never to *be* angry out loud. Always maintain calm. You want that class to be a happy place (Brian. i.8).

Teachers who made the class a happy place in one way or another are prominent in the memories of those who become teachers of teachers and are seen in retrospect as a key influence on later decisions to teach like Mr Marley in my story:

> He worked hard at building up a class community which I felt part of ... I did well at school (that year) and felt good about myself ... It was the first time I thought that being a teacher might be a pretty good job because Mr Marley was the first teacher I had met who seemed to really enjoy being a teacher (Mike.s.7).

Kay contrasts two teachers who had an influence on her own approach:

> The woman who taught French. She knew her stuff and she rattled it out. But if you couldn't keep up or were a bit slow or she took a dislike to you. She was really quite, well, unpleasant: curt, sarcastic, mocking even. She looked like she was feeling ill when some of us tried to speak French. It left its mark on me that face. I still can't speak French. Just can't make myself do it. But the music teacher, he made everyone believe they could sing. He was kind,

fun, good to be around. He encouraged everyone to have a go and I still do you know? I still sing all the time but I can't really hold a tune if I'm honest (laughing). When I started working with children I knew which of those two I wanted to be like. (Kay.i.5).

Brian recognises Mr Morgan as a central influence upon his own beliefs about teaching:

That was when I knew what I wanted to do I think. The room was like a learning lab. You couldn't walk in there without learning something. He didn't really have great social skills as far as I remember. He just took us off on this learning journey – in the real sense of the phrase – and if you chose not to go then that was up to you, that was your loss. He helped people but it was all about the knowledge, the information and what it meant. I knew that would be a great way to spend the day; helping people to find things out. (Brian.s.1).

Jan remembers the motivational influence of Miss Cox from secondary school:

She really made me want to be a teacher because she seemed to enjoy it so much. She was so good at it. I could see myself doing that. Thinking back it was also the way she taught and engaged with the class and loved the subject which had an influence on me. Probably more of an influence on me than any of my training or experience in some ways. (Jan.i.2).

Sian's strongest memory of recognising good teaching was as an undergraduate:

It was the first time I met someone who I thought was *outstanding*. I liked my (school) teachers, most of them anyway and they taught me well ... but they were, and this sounds a bit arrogant or ungrateful, the same as me; at that time rather provincial and normal. They seemed like my mother and my step-father. Good people, don't get me wrong but I suppose Daines and Preston (lecturers) seemed special, extra-ordinary. They were famous, published. Oh I'm beginning to sound like a groupie or something. (Sian.i.6).

The ways in which we construct memories of 'good' and 'bad' experiences of learning and of teachers has a direct influence upon how we idealise and demonise teachers and how we wish to teach and influence students preparing to teach. This also brings problems such as those that emerged for me as a teacher of seven year-olds when I was unable to live up to my own memories of Mr Marley and felt equally haunted by those of my bullying head teacher when I realised that:

While I certainly never hit or hurt anyone, several of the children in my class were frightened in various ways. They were desperate to please me or worried about upsetting me in case I became disappointed or angry with them. (Mike.s.18).

Similarly Jan felt increasingly unable to emulate her memory of Miss Cox who made learning about literature so exciting for her:

> Sometimes I remember thinking that I was teaching well and Miss Cox would be proud of me...
>
> ...early 90s the national curriculum started to kick in and then soon after that all the literacy stuff. That pretty much killed it for me ... the literacy strategy took all the fun out of it. I thought it would be OK at first but it wore me down. (Jan.i.5).

There is clearly a sense in which idealised memories of teachers form and support opinions of what it is to be a good teacher and that these influence how teachers then attempt to teach. This can lead to disappointment and to disaffection. The failure to teach up to these memories is often blamed upon changes in education or society such as Jan's assertion that the national literacy strategy more or less drove her out of school teaching or Brian's view that the OFSTED inspection system had damaged the teaching and learning at his school. A source of further disappointment for teacher educators can be the unwillingness of students to adopt some of the ideals which they have been motivated by themselves:

> Peter: I very rarely now see students who want to change the world. They say the right things. They are very kind and caring. Well – organised and efficient, but they don't have that passion and drive that's about more than their careers.
>
> Mike: Do you think that's about confidence? That it might come later?
>
> Peter: You need the passion first. It's what gets you through. Why do it otherwise? Teaching I mean. You can't teach passion. You've either got it or you haven't (Peter.i.14).

Passion for teaching may appear in many ways of course but Peter links it closely to his memories of being a pupil and of being a teacher in further education. He finds little evidence of this particular form of passion for teaching in his students.

Other Voices

Many forms of passion and learning also emerge and are engendered from reading literature. The rather strange influence of Emmett Grogan's (1972) dubious autobiography upon me reflects my own state of mind and perceived situation at the time of reading to a large extent and is similar in some ways to Jan's and to Peter's feelings about Steinbeck's *The Red Pony* (1933/1976) and Hardy's *Far From the Madding Crowd* (1874/1965) respectively. Identifying with a character in autobiographies, short stories or novels is often part of the rights of passage process for adolescents. My own interest in Grogan's far away life was another form of escape from what I saw as the ordinariness of my own life. The location and lifestyle seemed exotic and different and the character seemed to allow me to succeed without

CHAPTER 5

conforming. I aspired to something different and although the violence and sexism of Grogan's story now appals me I can see how I identified and wanted to identify with the idea of the intellectual outlaw and how this continues to influence my thinking. Jan identified with Jody in *The Red Pony* when she was 14 because he seemed to be like her. She recognised a kindred spirit in a far away place and in a different time. Making a connection across time with Gabriel Oak in *Far From the Madding Crowd* meant a lot to Peter when he was 14:

> It seemed as though I was there with him. I *was* him in a way. I became part of the story as I read it and the story became part of my life and the way I saw the world (Peter.i.12).

Reading and story is a key element in all the life-histories gathered here. Sian did not identify a particular book or author as especially influential until she met two famous authors at university, but her interest and love of literature was clearly a key influence on her as a girl. Reading later became the conduit for a wider philosophy of poetics that she adopted in her 20s and which in turn influenced her work as a teacher and teacher-educator:

> I think the thing I took on, the 'torch' as I call it, is about learning and about life. A sort of view of the world. A poetic sort of way of understanding the world. I think I kept that from (Professor) Preston, from his poetry work, his work on poetry. And I've kept it myself in my own way in my own life. The way I see the world. That's what education's all about really isn't it? (Sian i.5).

Sian's notion of her professor 'passing on the torch to us and we would carry it on from there' (Sian.i.4), and Jan's idea of 'being a teacher of spreading the word' (Jan.i.3) reveal a perspective of teaching and learning as a 'passing on' of skills, values and knowledge from one generation to the next. Literature plays a particular role here for Sian and Jan and can also directly inform views on teaching, teacher identity and learning itself. Brian was influenced by Braithwaite's (1971) famous book:

> I'm a bit embarrassed about this but I have to admit that *To Sir with Love* had quite, the book not the film, had quite an influence on me. Even when I became a teacher I thought about it. The way he had to win the youngsters over, get their respect. I taught in a school like that in London. You couldn't do much until they were on your side (Brian.i.10).

Moving On

I stayed in the same town I grew up in until I was 46 but all the other participants had moved away before they were 25 and have never lived in their home towns again. Brian saw education as a means of escape from a place and a life he didn't want:

> My brother is a good example. He stayed there and ended up in all sorts of trouble. He could have done anything that I've done. I'm sure of that. He was just as bright. But he stayed on for one reason or another. Money really, and

when all the steel works shut he was done for. Things went from bad to worse (Brian.i.4).

For Brian, what he sees as his brother's fall is linked most clearly to his decision to stay in their home town in Wales and not pursue his education and his career elsewhere as Brian did. Sian also came to see her home town as a representing her pre-educated past:

I saved my own life. Education was the means of escape. You know yourself that there are still lots of people who live their parents' lives or try to. But their lives have gone away. I wanted something more (Sian.i.8).

Taking Sides: Choosing and Learning to Teach

The concept of 'sides' and the need to 'win them over' feature within all of the self-narratives here. As young learners we had different views of which side we were on and where the boundaries were drawn. My own pre-occupation and concerns about being controlled and dictated to hindered my education while I was at school but it later became a motivation and a way of seeking independence and distinctiveness: 'I wanted to succeed without conforming and I wanted to be different'(Mike.s.6).

Fears of the uncertainties of life were matched by a fear of the inevitability of the ordinariness of being like everyone else. Education changed for me in my early teens from being a way in which we were made to be the same into a way in which one could be different: 'I seemed to be finding a way to learn and to study and stay out of trouble without feeling controlled by others' (Mike.s.10).

So when the time came I found it easier to learn as an adult because I was there by choice and, to begin with at least, nothing much seemed to depend upon it. A friend described me as an 'autodidact' at some point in the 1990s, and there was a time, between school and signing up for 'O' levels at age 25 in 1984 when my learning was largely self-directed and self-organised. I read lots of books and often discussed them with no one else. I wrote poems and long entries in my diary and elsewhere that only I read. The need to share what I thought and knew and the need for interaction and guidance became stronger than the fear of rejection or being controlled and restricted. I stepped back towards formal education as I felt more confident as I sought an audience and a dialogue. I also felt the motivation, vague at first of wanting some qualifications to make a change in my life. I still see this as a sort of surrender. A final recognition that I wasn't going to San Francisco and that while today may have been the first day of the rest of my life I did need to think about the future. Peter remembers a similar sensation when he started his BEd at the age of 24:

Because my Mother and Father were a Head and deputy Head respectively, there was a sort of inevitability about me going into teaching which my family enjoyed a good deal. I had resisted the idea of being a teacher for six years. I worked for a publisher and then as a customs officer. I felt as though my options were open and that I might live and work abroad and that nobody knew what career I would eventually pursue. But when I did decide on a career it was teaching. I suddenly felt as though there was nothing else I could really do and that I should get on with it. My sister had gone straight to it: training then a job. I thought everyone would be surprised when I decided to apply for the BEd but far from it. There was an attitude of 'oh there you are at last Peter, we've been expecting you.' I felt pleased to be joining the fold in so many ways and I did have some real advantages – teachers everywhere, but I also had a sense of sadness; a sense of a sort of narrowing down of my options. I suppose that's all part of growing up but I don't think I was quite ready for that at the time. Perhaps that's why it all went wrong (Peter.s.2).

As in my own narrative Peter's concerns about being controlled were later mirrored by his discomfort at being in a position of control over others but I never felt any of the sense of inevitability or family expectation about becoming a teacher that he experienced.

My own options expanded in many ways when I started my degree course in humanities. Around 9% of UK 18–30 year olds went to university or polytechnic in 1987 (HESA, 2005) and less than 10% of those were from the 'working class' social economic groups 4,5,6 (DfEE, 1996) which is how I saw myself. But it was a rapidly decreasing currency as numbers went up and I needed to find a job as the course came to an end. Unlike Jan who looks back and sees that 'from about age 14 it was all I wanted to do' (Jan i.2), or even more so, Kay, who says she was born to be a teacher, I had little idea of what I wanted to do until I came to the end of my degree and rather like Peter 'felt as though there was nothing else I could really do'.

Sian identified teacher education as a possible future career before the end of her PGCE course and although she had already chosen the secondary science teaching route, she only decided to actually become a teacher while she was on the course: 'I had no idea if I really wanted to be a teacher. I was finding out. That was what I was doing, finding out if I wanted to be a teacher' (Sian.i.12).

Although she did well at school and gained excellent qualifications, Sian sees her time at university as the era of biggest change for her as a learner in a variety of ways:

> I found myself in some way. I was young and I did well. Got a first. Discovered sex. (I was) away from home for the first time and I felt good about myself for the first time (Sian.i.5).

Feeling good, or better, about myself took longer and happened up to a point outside of higher education. My mixed experiences of school and the abrupt exit, without any qualifications, from compulsory education made me feel that degrees were for other people. The reconstruction of my self-confidence and my journey from the bakery to the polytechnic can be gathered and traced in my narrative and viewed as another kind of bricolage of independent reading, private writing, chance encounters with students, encouragement from an old friend, the disappointments, disillusionments and then the catalyst of becoming a parent. Once I arrived at the polytechnic I was ripe for further change and I soaked it up like a sponge.

Brian was a high achiever throughout his time at school. He studied mathematics at university but music was his first love: 'I sang before I could talk and I was playing some sort of rhythm before I could walk' (Brian.s.1). His musical enthusiasm, knowledge and skills gave Brian a different view of the world from an early age: 'I thought about studying music and about being a professional musician for a while. That's probably why I moved to London after Oxford' (Brian.s.2). Maths and music were in stiff competition with each other for Brian's commitment during his university years but: 'In the end I went for maths but I'm not 'special' at maths which is why I became a school teacher. I felt that I could do some maths and some music there' (Brian.s.2).

Brian has some bad memories of his preparation for teaching as part of his Cert Ed:

> 'It was grim I can tell you. Theory without practice. Some of the lectures we had (shakes his head). Renowned academics who hadn't been in a school for years, if ever. We learnt it all on teaching practice – those who survived. I remember at my school. It's been closed down now it was that bad. I gave a boy detention and members of his family came to the school to beat me up at the end of the day. The caretaker showed me the back way out of the school through a hole in the fence. Nothing about calling the police. When I got back to college I asked them how they would handle a situation like that. They said I'd done the right thing but the police should be informed and asked to warn the family to stay away. Can you imagine? No idea. (Brian.i.9).

Peter was to take a more circuitous route to teacher education:

> I failed my second year placement and I just couldn't face it after that. The whole system seemed to be mean-spirited and all about controlling the kids. I felt as though I was being asked to police them I certainly couldn't control them and I dropped out of the course (Peter.i.16).

Through the three sections of Chapter 5 I have presented a narrative analysis based upon Sartre's progressive-regressive method (1963) and Denzin's critical interpretive framework (1997, 2001), aiming to examine the conceptual structures which inform the self-narratives and allowing the reader to consider how the cultural practices connected to structural formations are experienced by these interacting individuals within teacher education.

REFERENCES

Anderson, L. (2006). Analytic autoethnography. *Journal of Contemporary Ethnography*, 35, 373–395.
Ball, S. J. (2003). The teacher's soul and terrors of performability. *Journal of Education Policy*, 18, 215–228.
Braithwaite, E. R. (1971). *To sir, with love*. Oxford: Heinemann.

CHAPTER 5

Denzin, N. K. (1997). *Interpretive ethnography: Ethnographic practices for the 21st Century*. Thousand Oaks: CA, Sage.
Denzin, N. K. (2001). *Interpretive interactionism*. London: Sage.
DfEE. (1996). *Lifelong learning: A policy framework*. London: HMSO.
Ellis, C., & Bochner, A. P. (2000). Autoethnography, personal narrative, reflexivity: Researcher as subject. In N. K. Denzin, & Y. S. Lincoln (Eds.), *Handbook of qualitative research* (2nd ed.) 773-769 Thousand Oaks, CA: Sage.
Fiske, J. (1994). Audiencing: Cultural practice and cultural studies. In Denzin, N. K., & Lincoln, Y. S. (Eds.), *Handbook of qualitative research* 189-198 Thousand Oaks, CA: Sage.
Goodson, I. F. (Ed.). (1992). *Studying teachers lives*. London: Routledge.
Goodson, I. F. (2003). *Professional knowledge, professional lives: Studies in education and change*. Maidenhead: Open University Press.
Grogan, E. (1972). *Ringolevio: A life played for keeps*. London: Heinemann.
Hardy, T. (1965). *Far from the madding crowd*. London. Macmillan: St. Martins Press.
Higher Education Statistics Agency. (2005). http://www.hesa.ac.uk/index.php/component/option,com_datatables/ltemid,121/. Last accessed on 2nd May, 2011.
Kelchtermans, G. (1993). Teachers and their career story: A biographical perspective on professional development. In C. Day, J. Calderhead, & P. Denicolo (Eds.) *Research on teacher thinking: Understanding professional development* 198-220 London: Falmer, Routledge.
Munro, P. (1998). *Subject to fiction: Women teachers' life history narratives and the cultural politics of resistance*. Buckingham: Open University Press.
Polkinghorne, D. (1995). Narrative configuration in qualitative analysis. In Hatch, A., & Wisniewski, R. (Eds.), *Life history and narrative* 5-23 London: Falmer.
Sartre, J. -P. (1963). *The problem of method*. London: Methuen.
Sartre, J. -P. (1981). *The family idiot: Gustave Flaubert, 1821–1857, Vol. 1*. Chicago: Chicago University Press.
Sikes, P. J., Measor, L., & Woods, P. (1985). *Teacher careers: Crises and continuities*. London: Falmer.
Steinbeck, J. (1933/1976). *The red pony*. Harmondsworth: Penguin.
Vygotsky, L. S. (1978). *Mind in society: The development of higher psychological processes*. Cambridge, MA: Harvard University Press.

CHAPTER 6

SOME CONCLUSIONS

POLYTECHNIC AND UNIVERSITY

I took the lorry out to the polytechnic for an interview during my lunch break in March 1987 and it seemed like another world. I thought it would be hard to get in but the interview went well and I realised about half way through the discussion with Dr Boxall that he was telling me what I would be doing when I started the BA in Humanities course. When I asked him if I definitely had a place on the course he seemed surprised: "Oh yes, I thought you knew that. I thought you'd come for a chat before you decided" he said. "Decided what?" I asked "Where you were going" he answered. I took the place and cried a bit when I got back to the lorry. I was very conscious of a new beginning and a chance to change my life after twelve years of manual work. I had not realised how much I wanted the place until I knew I had it. I also knew that things would never be the same again, and they were not.

I did well at the polytechnic which became a university. I was ready to study and to write and I enjoyed pretty much all of it. I made some good friends. For a while early on I felt as though I was in a sort of social limbo, not part of the younger student group who were fresh out of sixth form and no longer part of the old crowd at the pub. They thought I had lost my mind going 'back to school' and that I ought to at least do something useful like a government training course where I could learn a trade. My wife and my mother were not sure either. They were keen on the idea of education but no one in our families had ever taken a degree and it was not clear where a degree in humanities would lead to for a father of two. I had no idea where it was leading either. As the first year came to an end I wondered for a while what all this study meant in my life and I found a way to connect my past to my present through the community writing and publishing group that I joined and helped to organise and run from 1988. The course seems to have passed quickly and it began or increased changes and widened the distance between me and some others especially my wife whose family were particularly sceptical and generally amused that I was now a student. I think they thought I was getting above myself.

I was certainly starting to see myself in a different way as I progressed through the course. I did not know what I might do when I finished but I knew that I would have to work to support my family. I was not aware of considering teaching until the beginning of my last undergraduate year but I wonder now if it had been at the back of my mind since primary school when I thought that Mr Marley seemed to be having a good time. I went back into a primary school for the first time in a long time when my son started school. Like most parents I didn't feel very comfortable but I didn't have to leave him in the playground on his first day and he was much happier at school than I had been. The publishing group I worked with held an event at the school to launch the autobiography of a man who had started as a pupil there in 1919. He came to talk to the children and I was struck by how enthusiastic and interested they were. It was a very enjoyable and friendly occasion. I think it put teaching back at the forefront of my mind as a possibility and made me see it beyond my own experience as a pupil. When I went for a career aptitude computer assessment at the careers department I remembered that I had been a fork lift truck instructor at the carpet company and that I had been a coach at the running club when I was a member in the early and mid-eighties. Teaching came up as my most likely career choice given my stated interests, qualifications and experience although I had not told the computer that I had been expelled from school. I began the primary PGCE at the same polytechnic in 1990 still not knowing how much I wanted to be a teacher and if I could really do it. 15 years later I came back to the same rooms at what was now the university and started teaching on the PGCE. Being a student on the PGCE persuaded me that I wanted to have a go at teaching. It allowed me to believe that I could be a good teacher and enjoy it. I made connections between the sort of community politics and activities I was involved with, a developing philosophy of personal growth and change leading to social change, and working in a school. Social class and politics had been a prominent theme in my BA studies, my work with the writing group, the local labour party and now the PGCE. In a further return to my roots I did my final school teaching placement in the area where I grew up and where my mother still lives, although thankfully not at my old school. I taught several children of people I had been at school with. They were always surprised but always apparently pleased that I was working with their children. One of them said "it's like they've taken you away and done something to you." I was offered a job at the school providing I passed the placement and the course.

On the morning I passed my final observation and therefore the course I found myself on my own in the classroom while the children sang in assembly. I could hear them singing "Forgive our foolish ways" [ii]in the hall along the corridor. I looked out over that side of town. I could see my old school to the south and the window I used to look out of when I was ten, and across the valley the hospital where my mother worked and my father died. I could see the house where I now lived with my own family and the school my sons went to. Above all this on the brow of the hill to the west I could see the bakery – still a bakery in 1991 I think – and then to the north, along that road, the polytechnic I was about to leave and the university I would return to in another 15 years. At the time, with the children's voices singing of human weakness and divine forgiveness it felt like the end of a journey. All the pieces seemed to be there in front of me with a few sections out of sight like a puzzle that had not been put together.

CONCLUSIONS: THE PROFESSIONAL LIFE AND WORK OF TEACHER EDUCATORS

In this chapter I evaluate how using this experimental approach allowed me to investigate my subject and my method and examine the reciprocal and recursive relationships between memory of experience, identity and practice within the professional life and work of teacher educators. I discuss some of the implications for educational research, the practice of teacher education, and for me.

Another Story in the Story

I set out through this research to make a study of the professional identity of university-based teacher educators. Motivated to understand my own experience and believing that valuable insights are gained by examining how narrative both forms and represents identity, I took the 'narrative turn' and found my route through the field, guided by my version of an analytic autoethnography.

My autoethnographic expedition for understanding how narratives of experience form and represent professional identity for myself and my colleagues did not take me to new, sturdy definitions and methods for establishing absolute truth. It did lead me to a deeper understanding of teacher education and autoethnography that I believe contributes towards professional knowledge in a number of ways. It also led me back to teacher education as a full-time profession. Exploring the experience of becoming and being a teacher educator from a number of perspectives and contexts in studying the profession for the first time gave me a new, clearer, more positive perspective of the role and of myself. I am learning and teaching again within a university school of education and this time it will be different.

The 'I' in my story has become also part of the 'us' in our story. Writing and sharing my telling tale gave me a new perspective on my own story. I knew the story well but found new understandings as I wrote it, then further understanding as I heard others respond to it through stories of their own. I found a story of myself within the stories of becoming and being teacher educators. So it will be different this time because I have found, indeed constructed, a community of experience within which I can now situate my own experience and continue to develop my perspective and professional identity. This allows me to see the role of teacher educator in a different way. Gaining insights through this research into how we construct our understandings of the roles of learners, teachers and teacher educators and how this influences our professional identities, now allows me to take on new, more productive perspectives. On an everyday, individual level this will mean that I frame my working experience and practice within a context that both informs and supports me. The bad day at work is still a bad day at work but it rarely undoes me as it once seemed to. This clearly has collective as well as individual applications for teacher educators in reclaiming and developing the profession through new understandings of the role and pedagogy of teacher education. Memory emerging as narrative within the professional lives of teacher educators could be one means of asserting our professional identity and authority against the discourses of institutional power as the current wave of politically driven change in education gathers momentum. This is an important area of research with a rich a seam of evidence in teacher education at a time when the profession again comes under fiscal and ideological pressure.

CHAPTER 6

The accounts reported in this book are subjective versions of becoming and being a teacher educator. I am conscious that multiple readings and interpretations can be made of the accounts I have organised through the themes of Chapter 5 that emerged from the writing and sharing of self-narratives and interviews. My central concern has been upon what Bruner (1990, p.137) calls 'meaning-making' and how it connects with what he terms 'folk psychology', within initial teacher education. So to conclude my route I need to look back at the journey represented by this book and consider the meaning I make of it. Returning to Raymond Carver's (1990) definition of the writer's task suggests the question of what news from one world does this narrative bring to another? What can this story tell you about what I have learnt and how does this inform professional knowledge in educational research and in teacher education? The news is about the method as much as the field as this book traces my experimental approach to exploring these subjects. To tell the story of the journey I need of course a voice drawn from the toolbox of autoethnography, the bricolage of methods and voices I have gathered and used along the way, and that voice is my own.

My belief that the examination of the construction of our own memories and identity through narrative discourse is a source of rich description and insight was deepened and reinforced through this work. The processes by which we articulate our selfhood as educators of teachers through stories of our own experience and how this informs the development of our professional identities is illuminated for examination through for example my own self-narrative and the narrative analysis of Chapter 5. These glimpses and patches demonstrate how experience is continually construed and re-construed as our lives are constructed, not recorded, through the different forms of self-narrative. The telling of the tale itself becomes part of our experience informing who we think we are. Thus we remain in the middle of these stories which develop in a relational dialogue with our developing understanding of the context within which they are set. The critical moments, conversions, awakenings, turning points, emerge in the process of writing self-narrative and form key passages that are recognised by and stimulate responses in others.

Our professional identities continue to evolve in response to the changing nature of teacher education in England. By engaging with and drawing together the relevant literature and research of teacher education and the methodology of memory, I was able to establish a foundation from which to develop a theoretically informed understanding of how the professional identity of these teacher educators *is* both formed and represented by such narratives of experience. The narrative analysis reveals some common themes that we share among our stories of experience. These are the points where our stories intersect and a shared influence, desire or decision can be recognised and linked to earlier influence, beliefs and decisions: the beliefs of our parents; stories of sibling triumphs and troubles; the need for approval; the need to escape; becoming a teacher; struggling and/or thriving as teacher educators. These themes are represented and organised within the headings and subheadings of Chapter 5 based upon my analysis and my interpretation of the data.

SOME CONCLUSIONS

While sharing my story with the other participants had an influence by design, and not withstanding significant individual differences, I was surprised by how similar many aspects of our stories appear to be, and how many values and beliefs about teaching and learning and the education of teachers we share with each other. On reflection this is of course not surprising at all given that our experiences have been shaped within a broadly similar era of education policy. Many of our common experiences as learners, for example, relate closely to the policy contexts of the time such as the long post-war 'consensus' on education as a means of social improvement, the eleven plus, the comprehensive system, the first and second waves of widening participation in Higher Education and what can be fairly described as the theoretically and research-informed teacher education policies of the 1970s and early 1980s, at least as compared to more recent policy. While our length of professional experience varies, we were all learners at points within that era as we were as teachers within the turbulent and often personally shredding era of school reform that began in the late 1980s. Our experiences differ but we were all part of that time. When considered from this perspective it is the differences between us that seem surprising. Our individual stories and, what Goodson (1992, 2003) calls our 'genealogies of context' blend and mix here to make the larger picture where our unique shades of identity can be drawn from the palettes of experience that we often share.

So Who Do We Think We Are and What Do We Think We Do?

The self-narratives and discussions around the questions of who we are as teacher educators revealed a number of issues concerning self-image. While our own assessments of the quality of our work as teacher educators vary there is a common perception which runs through the data that we are falling short of the ideal. The gap between self-image and ideal self-image often seems wide for these teacher educators. Participants identify the structures they work within leading to an overload of work, along with external requirements and constraints as the main causes of this. Confusion about our role, especially during the early years in post is a further factor identified by all participants. People talked about feeling de-skilled and losing their identity as teachers as their school or college teaching experience became more distant. Most have found new ways of framing and connecting their past experience and skills to their present roles but even the most experienced teacher educators feel uncertain about their role at times and find it difficult to keep up with research and policy while managing their commitment to teaching students.

Significantly, none of us wished to return to teaching in a school or college although we have all considered it. Our reasons included negative developments in schools and colleges themselves, reluctance to take backward steps and a perceived lack of intellectual challenge in school teaching. This is an implicit acknowledgment, of some of the rewards of working in ITE which most participants made explicit at various points as seen in Chapter 5.

CHAPTER 6

Everyone agreed that working in ITE can be a rewarding and satisfying job but that there was a gap between how we wanted to teach and how we actually taught. Teaching about teaching in a way that often seems to contradict *what* we are teaching makes us acutely aware of this gap. Motives for becoming teacher educators revealed through the interviews and stories are inextricably linked within this group to becoming teachers at an earlier point in their careers. Views of the idealised or demonised teachers and head teachers of our childhood contribute towards motivation and job satisfaction but they can also undermine it as when Jan states that she felt she was letting her teacher down by teaching the literacy hour or my fears that I might be turning into my head teacher from primary school.

Student results remain important here but they do not correspond as closely with motivation and job satisfaction in ITE as pupil results do for school teachers. They continue to provide a sense and a measure of professional competence that these teacher educators both regard and resent. Relationships with colleagues are most significant as is the perceived support one gets from the head of school. An important contributing theme towards dissatisfaction is the perceived decreasing social status of teacher educators; a process likely to accelerate as current government policy develops towards strategies of school-based apprenticeship models of ITE in England.

The content of the job as perceived by the teacher educators links closely to the concept of dilemma since the question is not only what must a teacher educator do but what must we do to be effective teacher educators? This altered significantly during participants' careers and is closely linked to external as well as to experiential influences. Structure, culture and the individual meet with the past and the future here in contributing to new understandings.

Change and development in self-image, job satisfaction and the perception of role that teacher educators expect to take place, form a central component of our professional selves. The orientation towards the future is implicitly present in the professional self and therefore forms a background against which teacher educators make decisions in their professional lives and work.

Autoethnography: The me in My Methodology

Experimenting with these methods of research was rewarding, exciting and liberating, but never settling or reassuring. I came to understand and agree with Schon's (1971) point that all real change and learning involves feelings of 'being at sea, of being lost, of confronting more information than you can handle' (p.12). While the data and discussions from this investigation illuminate several of the key issues about becoming and being a university-based teacher educator in the first decades of the 21st Century it is clearly not the purpose of autoethnography or life-history research to identify universal processes or generalisations. My approach has been to deliberately focus on individuals and to engage in an intensely personal type of research process. The feeling of being at sea did not go away but rather I developed some 'sea legs' and learnt to move and think in a way that allowed new types of understanding to emerge. Through this process of research and writing

I found new ways of living and working with uncertainty. The methods I have used illuminate the often hidden and private experiences that give meaning to everyday life, making things more visible without making them simple. In some ways I think this is enough as the reader, the audience, make meaning from the way we tell the story. The stories themselves have an evocative validity as they bring the news of experience and response from one person's world to another.

I had a particular doctoral destination to consider for my original research. I adopted Anderson's (2006) proposals for analytic autoethnography as a way of developing and framing my methodology in relation to more traditional ethnographic qualitative research. Although this sometimes felt like an uneasy compromise I was able to develop a version of analytic autoethnography that follows Anderson's five principles without surrendering my deepening commitment to an interpretive, narrative perspective: (1) I have been a **complete member researcher** within teacher education; (2) I followed and demonstrated the self-conscious introspection of **analytic reflexivity** through my writing; (3) I am a **highly visible** social actor within this text as my own feelings and experiences are incorporated into the story and form a key part of the data and the method; (4) the process of sharing stories and interviews with the other participants has ensured **a dialogue with informants beyond my self;** and (5) I demonstrate a commitment to **theoretical analysis** in using the progressive/regressive method of interpretation and presentation of my narrative analysis.

The advantage of access to and familiarity with the field that being a complete member researcher affords autoethnography is clearly one of its strengths. Access to my own and others 'insider meanings' allowed me to provide perspectives of a culture in action that would have been unavailable through other approaches. Analytic autoethnography specifically addresses the risk of author saturation and solipsism by situating and engaging others in the field. There are also practical and opportunistic advantages of being in the field for long periods of time and linking research aims with other activities such as teaching. I was able to combine and meld my research with part-time work activities in schools and universities during this study. However my earlier attempts at research foundered as I was overwhelmed by work commitments and began to associate the research itself with that stress. As well as being a way of understanding your own practice, there is always the potential danger that when things go badly the research can become just one more problem to face for complete member researchers.

Autoethnography offers opportunities to examine and analyse the connections between self-narrative and social structures in distinctively grounded ways. The narrative analysis here traces the ways in which the participants draw upon our personal experiences and perceptions to develop and describe our professional selves while simultaneously drawing on our social and professional understandings to enrich our understanding of our selves. These methods have allowed me to consider the connection and character of teacher educators' biography and pedagogy in new and illuminating way.

In some ways the limitations of autoethnography are closely related to its virtues. We clearly cannot only and always research and describe that in which we

CHAPTER 6

are personally or professionally entwined. Ethnographers will sometimes plan their research as professional strangers in order to research beyond direct biographical involvement, although I would argue that this connection is made when research begins and needs to be considered and made transparent as part of the research itself from that point on. While I now believe that autoethnographic thinking should influence all qualitative research I recognise that autoethnography is not the only toolbox in the workshop.

A CONTRIBUTION TO PROFESSIONAL KNOWLEDGE IN THE PRACTICE OF TEACHER EDUCATION

In this final section of the book I want to return to the story I began with and examine the ways in which the experience of writing and analysis has impacted on my own learning, professional practice and research sensibility, and to extend the discussion concerning autoethnography as a tool for teaching and reflective practice.

> The final rule: no text can do everything at once. The perfect ethnography cannot be written (Denzin, 1997 p287)

The complex work of teaching about teaching demands much of teacher educators. Sophisticated understandings of the relational nature of experience, identity and practice are needed to draw productive resources from this complexity. I believe that a process of writing, sharing, talking and listening that draws recursively upon perceptions of personal experiences to inform our understandings of our work as educators and upon our understanding of education to enrich our self-understandings makes a significant contribution to the development of professional knowledge and pedagogy in teacher education. As the focus of self-study in teacher education practice widens from students of teaching to include teacher educators themselves (Russell and Loughran, 2007; Heston et al., 2008) my approach offers a model for further collaboration and self-study between practitioners. It contributes to the growing momentum for the development and articulation of pedagogies of teacher education beyond apprenticeship. This offers exciting possibilities for on-going projects within and between schools of education that could easily and fruitfully extend across all sorts of borders in developing conceptual depth.

This research and writing has given me a personal and professional understanding that I believe allows me to work within and develop my professional knowledge and practice in teacher education. Using methods of self-study and sharing experiences with others has been a way of examining my self within a subculture and aspects of that subculture and the wider culture within my self. The perspective provided by the process offers me a way forward in my work as a teacher educator that connects past experience and present mind with future plans and action. I may have found the beginning of that new path to the waterfall after all.

One of the things that I have found most interesting and exciting about using and reading narrative research, analysis and writing is the way in which it continues, like identity itself, to grow, to shift and to develop even as it is constructed, and how this also continues beyond the writing, the typing and the printing of a book such as this. On the other hand one of the biggest difficulties in making shared meaning and drawing agreed conclusions from a project and a book like this is the way in which, it continues, like identity itself, to grow, to shift and to develop even after it is written and printed. Important as I think it is, I now realise that there is a real sense in which this type of approach fits uneasily into the traditional framework of the Doctoral thesis: the aims might seem vague, the methods can be seen as self-indulgent and the conclusions, well there are no 'real' conclusions. The whole thing might appear to be observational, partial, personal, and almost private. Narrative interpretive inquiry challenges the traditional categories themselves although I see no reason that it cannot simply extend our understanding of research into professional lives as it offers a new language of differing perspectives, sensibilities and reflexivity.

The research and writing that I have engaged with has opened not closed the discussion for me as I hope it will for others who read it in all its incompleteness. We learn different things when we read. Readers find different things and interpret data in different ways, making different meanings. People ask different questions and note different insights, absences, strengths and concerns. My supervisors understood the thesis in different ways, my examiners were concerned about particular omissions and subjects raised but not followed through as I pursue my own concerns sometimes narrowly through the chapters. The narratives in this book move backwards and forwards but they do not reach permanent and fixed destinations or come together to conclude neatly with generalisations or universal truths which can then be neatly applied to practice in teacher education.

When I read the original thesis in preparation for this book it seemed to have moved on in some way to tell a different story from the one I thought I had written. For me this indicates how the 'genealogy of context' (Goodson, 1992) continues to progress, to develop and to shift in meaning and significance. As a reader as well as writer I remain in the middle of the story. The story that my own story tells me continues to change and to develop as I and the profession of teacher education continue to change and develop.

We see different things, note different omissions depending upon our own perspectives. The key thing for me is how the participants perceive their own experiences, how they construct the stories they tell and the significance that they hold for them. I am therefore always missing the obvious point, but what that obvious point is, varies between readers as it varies between the participants. One reader felt there was a lack of a political analysis, another saw some interesting and central psychological leads that had been ignored. The participants themselves felt they had been heard and well-represented in the short profiles and the narrative analysis although they did not all agree with my own position and analysis of teacher education and educational research. 'Writers', as Joan Didion put it, 'are always selling somebody out' (Didion, 1968 p.xiv).

I believe that these stories are incomplete, fragmented and partial because all stories are. I know that my narrative analysis is incomplete and partial as all

CHAPTER 6

analysis is. I am sure that the current book is incomplete as that is the way books are. This data and these methods continue to offer some particular and personal glimpses into the experiences of working in ITE. They contribute towards my own clearer, more positive perspective towards the profession and help to make a connection with others in recognising a community of those who do this for a living. This offers the potential for others to use it in the same way while recognising the complexity of the contexts in which we develop our understandings.

I have not quite managed to live consistently comfortably with uncertainty through each academic year. Working in Initial Teacher Education remains a challenging, stressful although often rewarding job for all the reasons discussed in this book. Knowing why can help, but not always. Perhaps that is just the way this work, or all work, is. I should really know that by now.

Research and writing has helped me to work in new ways with students. I have used versions of self-narrative with students in getting them to reflect upon and analyse their own experiences of learning and teaching and to consider how this informs and will inform their practice. I worked with final year students as they used the progressive/regressive method to identify events from the course that they were about to complete, consider the significance of these for their work in schools and then make links with corresponding educational policies and initiatives. This brought a number of things to the surface including areas where students felt less prepared. The biggest response was in supporting the soon to be teachers to recognise how far they had come and what the key events were for them. The students were able to share their responses and analysis with each other in small groups allowing them to consider shared and differing perspectives in relation to their own analysis.

I remain convinced that autoethnography can be used in a number of ways in teacher education. I see autoethnography as a way to employ reflection in study and practice with significantly enhanced self-visibility. Understanding how what we know, what we feel and what we do informs, makes and remakes our pedagogy allows us to understand, adapt, respond and remake again. Autoethnography offers a way to situate the self within the teaching process as it allows us to situate the self in the research and writing process. This combines an individual's personal story with his or her scholarly story in an attempt as Burnier (2006) puts it to erase the false dichotomy between the scholarly and the personal where 'the actual scholar is embodied and present, as he or she examines closely the personal, political and scholarly situations that have shaped his or her life' (p412).

Blending the personal and the scholarly may be easier in the seminar room than on the published scholarly page within ITE but it is the combination of the personal and scholarly or indeed the evocative and the analytical that appeals to me as both teacher and researcher. At its best autoethnography provides both descriptive and theoretical insight. There is a danger, which I acknowledge that it can become solipsistic and self-indulgent but it holds real value for students if they are supported to be analytical and theoretical in its use and crucially in my view, if connections are made with the experiences of others.

Central to analytic autoethnography as proposed by Anderson (2006) is the notion that the personal story is subordinate to the larger empirical-theoretical story. While I attempted to follow this approach I remain torn on this point. Anderson's characterisation of two types of autoethnography can be seen as an attempt to contain, limit and silence the personal or the self. I do share Anderson's (2006) view that social science writing should not slip into narcissistic self-absorption and I understand that he is not proposing that analytic autoethnography encompasses the entire range of autoethnographic practices: 'There is indeed a wide range of ways in which self-study may yield valuable analytic insights' (Anderson, 2006 p446). We clearly cannot learn only from the particular events of our own lives. One of the defining features of analytic autoethnography whether used for teaching or in research is that it requires dialogue with others. This enables the researcher, teacher and/or student to identify a range of cognitive, emotional and behavioural understandings within the phenomena they are seeking to understand. Dialogue with others also provides a site for reflective engagement where different perspectives can challenge and enrich the researcher/teacher/student's own perspective and deepen analytic insights.

Anderson (2006 p463) argues that the most effective way to convince scholars of the value of analytic autoethnography is to exemplify it in actual practice. This applies to its use in teaching and learning as well as research and writing. This book is my latest attempt to exemplify a version of this approach. My next will be as part of my work in the education of those who wish to teach in the coming years.

Teaching

I think I became a good teacher. That's what all the appraisals and inspectors said over the years. I certainly carried on learning and became more confident. By the time I moved on to teach at the local infants' school after four years at the juniors I had developed my skills and come to believe that evaluating, reflecting upon and developing my own approach were the key skills for me as a teacher. But I never did completely get rid of the feeling that someone might come into the classroom and ask me what I was doing there and tell me to leave. While the critical reflection which I further developed during the MA in Education that I took with the Open University, helped me to develop my practice, it also fed my insecurity about the whole process of school teaching and learning and my place within it. This was largely about me and my own experiences of school: as well as being excluded from secondary school I had also failed in a number of ways as a learner. There were large gaps in my knowledge and skills. Also, while teaching within a mile of where I was born and grew up sometimes gave me a sense of progress and triumph over the past, it also served as a constant reminder of that feeling of failure and some of the pain of my childhood and youth. This in turn fed into my mixed feelings about schools and the education system. The 1990s were a time of increased regulation, prescription and proscription for teachers. The National curriculum led on to the Literacy Hour and the Numeracy Hour with headteachers and local authority advisors dancing to the OFSTED tune. The preparations for the

CHAPTER 6

three inspections I was involved with in mainstream schools dominated school activities for months and drove senior management and some staff to, and in one case beyond, the point of breakdown.

Generally I enjoyed the work in class. I felt that it mattered, and now it did matter, sometimes too much, that it was me. I tried to be fair and kind and gentle. I tried to encourage independence in the children but there was something about the system that put me in a position of control. It was more than making decisions and organising the teaching. I had to exercise control over the children and it bothered me from time to time. Sometimes it felt as though the teachers were planning and trying to control what the children thought as well as what they did. I felt a tension and a contradiction between the possibilities of facilitating learning in open ways and the teacher's role and responsibilities of controlling learning in narrow ways with defined outcomes. I turned to education for some answers again with the MA where I studied language and literacy, child development and gender in a social context. But this added to my questions. I could see the ways in which pressure and stress as well as values are passed down the line from politicians to children and the part that teachers play in that process. I was able to research, examine and write about this but I never managed to change it within my own situation at key stage 2 or key stage 1. I affected a rather individual approach arguing against regimentation and formulaic curriculum content and teaching strategies but in practice I pretty much followed the manual and measured myself as a teacher in a similar way to everyone else.

When a child accused me of striking them I was suspended from my job for two weeks while an investigation took place. On the way home I bumped into an old school friend who immediately joked "have they kicked you out again Mick?" I was not kicked out as the allegation was proved false or rather 'could not be proven' as the letter from the local authority put it. The incident made me realise that while I certainly never hit or hurt anyone, several of the children in my class were frightened in various ways. They were desperate to please me or worried about upsetting me in case I became disappointed or angry with them. This had a lot to do with them and their own circumstances of course but it was also a key part of the primary school system and my own classroom strategy. It mattered that it was me but not in the way I had wanted it to and I wondered if I was so different from my old head teacher just down the road.

Working as a teacher and advisor with children who were either outside or at the margins of the mainstream system gave me further opportunity to reflect upon what happens to some children and their families in schools. Teachers often saw me as the person who would 'deal' with the children with emotional and behavioural difficulties. They listened to advice and adapted their work and classrooms to support children but once a child had been referred to our service or become part of our school it was clear that there had been a shift in responsibility and there was often no way back into the mainstream. So I found myself at the edge of the system again. Working with children who did not fit in, trying to find ways forward through the maze of the education system not only for children and their parents, but also for me as a teacher. It was rewarding, if often stressful work. I taught a small group of excluded children in the special school primary department in the morning and then went out to several different schools in town to support children who were at risk of exclusion and their teachers. I did some work with secondary students and I signed up for a Professional Doctorate in Education at the university. The special school and support service that I worked for did not exist until 1978. It occurred to me that I might well have been one of those secondary students if it had been around in 1975. I am still not sure whether this would have helped me or not in the long term. Few of the young people who we supported were able to access and enjoy mainstream school in the 'normal' way and there was a certain amount of expectation and dependency from both children and the teachers we worked with. I began to wonder again if I was as much part of the problem as I was part of the solution.

I took on some part-time initial teacher-education work at the university teaching a module about inclusion and I loved it. It seemed to offer the perfect combination of ideas into practice that I had been struggling with. It felt strange and exciting to be back in the same rooms that I had worked in as an undergraduate and where I did my own teacher training. I felt very positive and authentic and knew what I wanted to do for a job at last. When I started a full-time job in the school of education at the university it felt like coming home. And so it was. But coming home is often a mixed experience and it did not work out for me.

At the university I had the unusual experience of becoming less confident the longer I worked there and I felt less and less authentic as the months went by. While I had felt like part of the problem in the education system to some extent as a school teacher and as an advisor I always felt that I was contributing something positive as well; something that some of the children would benefit from at some time. I used to call this 'nourishment': the knowledge that what one is doing is something worthwhile and making a contribution. I got less and less 'nourishment' at the university until it felt as though the scales had tipped and I could not enjoy the parts of the job I had loved at first. There seemed like even less time to think and to reflect upon things although I was in the habit of doing that now. It may well have been better not to in a way but I was committed to finishing something I had started and it seemed like a betrayal of my beliefs about learning to turn away now that I had found a comfortable job. Not that it was very comfortable by the last year when I knew I had to leave, do something else and tell my tale in one way or another for better or for worse.

REFERENCES

Anderson, L. (2006). Analytic autoethnography. *Journal of Contemporary Ethnography*, 35, 373–395.
Bruner, J. (1990). *Acts of meaning*. Cambridge, MA: Harvard University Press.
Burnier, D. (2006). Encounters with the self in social science research: A political scientist looks at autoethnography. *Journal of Contemporary Ethnography*, 35, 410–418.

CHAPTER 6

Carver, R., Gentry, M. B., & Stull, W. L. (1990). *Conversations with Raymond Carver*. Jackson, MS: University Press of Mississippi.

Denzin, N. K. (1997). *Interpretive ethnography: Ethnographic practices for the 21st century*. Thousand Oaks: CA, Sage.

Didion, J. (1968). *Slouching towards Bethlehem*. New York: Farrar.

Goodson, I. F. (Ed.). (1992). *Studying teachers lives*. London: Routledge.

Goodson, I. F. (2003). *Professional knowledge, professional lives: Studies in education and change*. Open University Press: Maidenhead.

Heston, M. L., Tidwell, D. L., East, K. K., & Fitzgerald, L. M. (2008). Introduction, *The seventh international conference on self-study of teacher education practices. Pathways to change in teacher education: Dialogue, diversity and self-study* 173-177 Herstmonceux Castle, East Sussex: England S-Step/University of Northern Iowa.

Russell, T., & Loughran, J. (Eds.) (2007). *Enacting a Pedagogy of Teacher Education*. London, Routledge.

Schon, D. (1971). *Beyond the stable state*. Harmondsworth: Penguin.

NOTES

[ii] Dear Lord and Father of Mankind by John G. Whittier, 1872

APPENDIX 1

CHRONOLOGY OF SELECTED MAJOR EVENTS IN TEACHER EDUCATION, 1960–2010

1960: Three-year course introduced in England and Wales.
1963: Robbins Report on Higher Education.
1964: Council for National Academic Awards (CNAA) established.
1965: First Bed courses commenced.
1966: Government White Paper on Polytechnics published.
Weaver Report on Government of Colleges of Education published.
1967: Plowden Report recommended a full enquiry into teacher education.
1968: CNAA Education Committee set up. Education Act (government of colleges).
1969: Commons Select Committee included teacher education in its brief.
1970: Area Training Organisation Inquiry into Teacher Education initiated. DES Circular 30/70 on balance of training issued.
1972: James Report on Teacher Education and Training published (January). White Paper: *Education: A Framework for Expansion* published (December).
1973: Advisory Committee for the Supply and Training of Teachers (ACSTT) established for a trial five-year period.
1975: Cuts proposed in initial education numbers.
The colleges of Education (Compensation) Regulations approved in Parliament and Circular 6/75 published.
1976: National Association of Teachers in Further and Higher Education founded.
1977: Further closures of colleges of education and departments announced.
1978: DES proposes minimum English and mathematics for all future teachers.
1980: Advisory Committee for the Supply and Education of Teachers (ACSET) set up.
1981: The 'independent' Standing Committee for the Education and Training of Teachers (SCETT) established.
1982: National Advisory Body for Local Authority Higher Education established. Decisions announced on new reduced targets for public-sector teacher education establishments; no further intakes for ITE at ten public sector institutions.

APPENDIX

1983: University Grants Subcommittee rejects DES attempts to impose PGCE quotas.
Publication of Government White Paper *Teaching Quality*. Circular 3/83 introduced earmarked grants for INSET priorities.
ACSET makes recommendations on criteria for the approval of initial teacher training courses.

1984: Circular 3/84, criteria for the approval of Teacher Training courses published.

1989: Introduction of two new routes into teaching: the Licensed Teacher Scheme and the Articled Teacher Scheme.
Council for the Accreditation of Teachers (CATE) established Circular 24/89, new criteria for the approval of Teacher Training courses published.

1992: Unification of the University system.
Demise of CNAA.
Minister for education Kenneth Clarke announces radical shift in ITT.
Creation of the Office for Standards in Education (Ofsted)
DfE Circular 9/92 with emphasis on practical training published:

1993: Circular 14/93 with emphasis on school-based aspects of teacher training, new partnership between HEIs and schools, introduction of SCITTs and a competence-based model of ITT published.

1994: Creation of the Teacher Training Agency (TTA) replaces CATE.

1996: OFSTED framework for the inspection of ITT courses established.

1998: Government Green Paper: *Teachers Meeting the Challenge of Change* published.
Publication of Standards for the Award of Qualified Teacher Status.
Introduction of curricula for ITT; circular 4/98 *High Standards, High Stakes*. Establishment of a General Teaching Council for England and Wales (Teaching and Higher Education Act)
OFSTED framework for the inspection of ITT courses developed.

2000: Introduction of Skills tests (numeracy, literacy, ICT for all beginning teachers.

2001: Green paper *Building on Success* with section on 'reforming teacher education.'

2002: Publication of the revised standards for QTS.

2003: Workforce remodelling government initiative aimed at reducing teachers' workload by employing more unqualified classroom assistants.

2004: University top-up fees introduced, allowing universities to charge variable fees. The Children Act based on the 2003 green paper *Every Child Matters*.

2005: Training and Development Agency (TDA) replaces TTA.
White paper *14–19 Education and Skills* rejected most of 2004 Tomlinson Report's recommendations.

2007: Teaching 2020 paper setting out the government's vision for schooling in the future. Revised framework of professional standards for teachers published by the Training and Development Agency.

2010: White paper *The Importance of Teaching* indicates plans to increase the 'proportion of time trainees spend in the classroom, focusing on core teaching skills, especially in reading and mathematics and managing behaviour. A network of Teaching Schools based on the model of teaching hospitals 'will lead the training and professional development of teachers'. Teaching schools will be outstanding schools which will take a leading responsibility for providing and quality assuring initial teacher training in their area.

2011: Consultation document *Training our next generation of outstanding teachers* sets out government proposals for the reform of 'initial teacher training.' Building upon ideas in the Schools White Paper, *The Importance of Teaching*. the document calls for schools to take greater responsibility in the system from 2012 encouraging them to lead their own initial teacher training in partnership with a university.

2011: New framework of standards for classroom teachers published by the Department for Education

APPENDIX 2

METHOD OF EXISTENTIAL PSYCHOANALYSIS

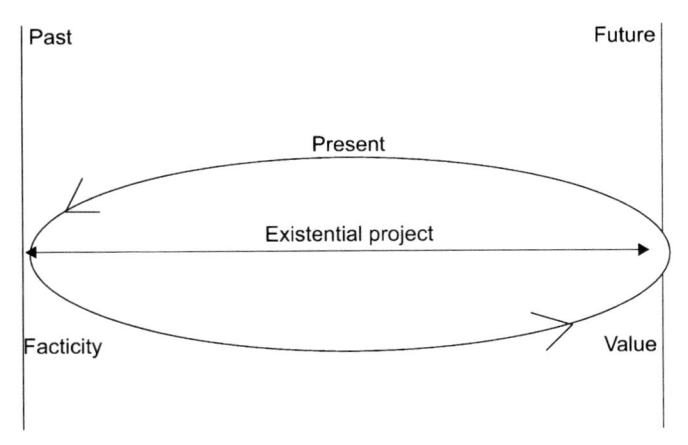

Farrar, R.C. (2000) Sartrean Dialectics: A Method for Critical Discourse on Aesthetic Experience, Amsterdam, Rodopi. Page 11